Girlfriend

Books by Barbara Henning

Poetry

Digigram, 2020
A Day Like Today, 2015
A Swift Passage, 2013
Cities & Memory, 2010
My Autobiography, 2007
Detective Sentences, 2001
Love Makes Thinking Dark, 1995
Smoking in the Twilight Bar, 1988

Novels

Just Like That, 2018
Thirty Miles to Rosebud, 2009
You, Me and the Insects, 2005
Black Lace, 2001

Other Prose

Poets on the Road, 2023 (with Maureen Owen)
Ferne, a Detroit Story, 2022

Editor

Prompt Book: Experiments for Writing Poetry and Fiction, 2020
The Selected Prose of Bobbie Louise Hawkins, 2012
Looking Up Harryette Mullen: Interviews on Sleeping with the Dictionary and Other Works, 2011

Girlfriend

BARBARA HENNING

Brooklyn, New York

Published by Hanging Loose Press,
PO Box 150608, Brooklyn, NY 11215.

Front Cover Design: HR Hegnauer
Cover Art: Julie Ezelle Patton
Interior Design: Norman Minnick
Author Photo: Michah Saperstein

www.hangingloosepress.com

Printed in the United States of America
10 9 8 7 6 5 4 3 2 1

Hanging Loose Press thanks the New York State Council on the Arts for a grant in support of the publication of this book.

ISBN: 979-8-9913377-0-0

CONTENTS

ACKNOWLEDGEMENTS

When my longtime yoga teacher, Genny Kapuler, read what I had written about her, she said, "I feel honored to be one of the beads in your mala, one of your sisters." I like to think of this book like that, as a poetic prose meditation on my friendships with girls and women. I started the project in the 1990s, writing some notes about childhood friends, and then I put it aside. This is a book that couldn't be written until later in life. A few years ago, when I returned to the project, I expanded it to include not only my adult friends, but also mentors and authors who were important during turning points in my life.

I am very thankful for all the men and women who over the years have offered support, love and friendship. I am especially thankful to the women who I write about in this book and the many who responded to drafts and provided photographs. I also want to thank others who offered encouragement and editorial feedback: Maria Damon, Maggie Dubris, Joe Elliot, Ed Friedman, Cliff Fyman, Bob Henning, Mitch Highfill, Jessica Caroline Holburn, Tony Iantosca, Arden Levine, Steve Levine, Kim Lyons, Laurie Price, Greg Masters, Gillian McCain, Elinor Nauen, Maureen Owen, Lisa Rogal, Bob Rosenthal, Michah Saperstein, Toni Simon, Michael Ruby and Don Yorty. Thanks also to the editors who published some of these short-shorts: Maureen Owen and Elinor Nauen at *Juleboard,* Jiwon Choi at *Hanging Loose Magazine;* Jamey Jones at *The Hurricane Review,* Jeff Wright at *Live Mag!,* Marjorie Tessor at *Mom Egg Review,* Amy Lutzke at *The Solitary Plover,* and Bill Lessard at *Heavy Feather Review.* A special thanks also to the designer, Norman Minnick, and the editors at Hanging Loose Press—Jiwon Choi, Joanna Fuhrman, Dick Lourie, Mark Pawlak, Elizabeth Hershon, and Thomas Moody—for their encouragement, support and careful attention to the text of *Girlfriend.*

LINDA

Two infants in the arms of two sisters. Two little girls at a big dining room table writing notes in a secret language. The streetcar rumbles past. Ooday ouyay havay aay igarettescay? Grandma smells a match. Under the covers you and I hide from the one we love most. Eight years old and hitchhiking on Alter Road. She pulls us back inside. We are only playing, we insist. She gives us what we never had at home—orange juice and blueberry muffins. Ten, eleven, twelve, we meet in the mall, and on the street, and I admire your performance of all the swear words in one long stream. '67, you are the bride. I am the maid of honor. Hair in a bouffant. Hair in a French twist. Lace and violets. Your garter, my garter. Your marriage. My rebel. Your drunk sailor, my sashaying pool shark. Your little girl, my little girl. The suburbs, the city, office work, teacher work. Many miles between us, but today you stretch out on my daybed, knitting little secret patterns, so adept with those needles, the scarf flowing over the edge of the bed and onto the floor. You look up at me writing in my notebook—"You and Bobby," you say, "could always read so fast."

Linda Bakke Matthew and Barbara. Left: 1954; right: 1967.

BRENDA & THE TWINS

You lived in a household of women, with your mother and grandmother. The twins lived in the house between ours. They were a little younger than we were. A cashier at Food Fair, their mother came home, made dinner, and while we were in the woods kissing Larry and starting little forest fires, all day long the twins had chores. We never went inside each other's houses. That was uncommon in the neighborhood. Instead, we carried on outdoors. Once we tore into each other with our nails because you said my father was an ass. Sometimes, we'd go behind the garage with our dolls or in a tent, and we'd play doctor. The twins' father was a big man, like a giant in a white dress shirt. When he told me they couldn't come out, he'd stand at the screen door and look down at me, sternly. I'd turn around on my heels and go home, not so sure about ever coming back.

Left: Brenda, 1960; right: the twins, 1958. Photos by Barbara.

DOT

We walked to Grant Junior High School together. Our houses were squat with unkempt yards inside chain link fences, both houses with a gang of kids inside running wild. Tall and short. Barb and Dot. Middle school hoodlums-in-mind-only with black short boots and tight skirts. I stole pantyhose from the dime store. You had an allowance. Huddled together in your bedroom, we stitched up the seams of my skirt, turned me into someone else. Soft brown hair now a wild nest smoothed over with hairspray. Thick black eyeliner. Two motherless girls. Mine died under an oxygen tent. Yours in the basement when a camp stove exploded. Stepmothers soon to arrive. I remember yours lounging around in her nightgown in the daytime with a glass of wine. Thirteen years old and arm in arm, preparing each other for the day ahead. When we walked down Nine Mile Road, it was *touch me,* but then, *don't dare touch me.*

Left: Dot, 1962; right: Barbara, 1963. *Grant Junior High School Yearbook.*

CINDER GIRL

I was a fighter. I fought with my stepmother. And my sisters were not my stepsisters, they were just like me. I did sleep in an attic room, like you, and so did my sisters, and we wore old clothes, hand-me-downs, not rags like yours. I would talk to my mother and pray to her, but no miracles, no magic birds, no golden shoes. When you grow up, dear, my mother said, you will have plenty of love and kisses. She meant a husband. I went for the plenty. In my bed in the attic by the hallway light, I read book after book, discovering utterly different worlds, but the problem was—how to get away, run away. One day a good-looking James Dean, with a tendency toward petty crime, came along in his souped-up car. Then another and another, but now I'm here with my words, my body and a big oak tree swaying in the wind. You, however, remain forever on the covers of many books, miraculously beautiful sitting by the side of your prince.

LAURA

When I think of you, I remember endless frightening winter, you and your family barely protected from predators, the fierce wind and that enormous, empty frozen snowbound prairie. As a child in a suburb of Detroit, I could hear the same wind outside my window, and I'd feel the same burn on my cheeks as I walked in the freezing cold, still dark in the morning, on my way to school, traffic minimal back then, the car lights shining on the snow as they passed me by. I had no doubt when I opened the door to our house, that the floor would be warm and at dinnertime, there would be food. Your family would sing together, loving even when wolves were howling outside a roughly built house without doors or windows. While eating only bread and tea, I wonder if you weren't sometimes a little impatient or irritated. Maybe a strap and a whack now and again. When it was bitter cold and your mother put you in a dress and scolded you, or the time she told you it was impolite for little girls to interrupt, you must have bit your lip or growled just a little—Didn't you?

Laura Ingalls, 1879 or 1880.

CINDY

You were the girl my mother wanted me to be. Get your Bible badge, follow the Girl Scout laws, be loyal, helpful, a friend to Girl Scouts and animals, obedient, thrifty, cheerful, clean in thought word and deed. Some afternoons, I'd do my algebra homework with you. Your sister had an Elvis Presley poster on her bedroom wall, and she had taken a bus to see his house, you said. Secretly, I used to gloat over your uncool innocence. You must have known. Once you took me to youth night at the Baptist church. When the preacher called everyone forward, all the teenagers started crying and gathering on stage. I sat in the middle of a row of empty folding chairs. "I'm a Lutheran," I whispered. You kneeled and then the men took you into the back room. I never knew what happened there, but you seemed pleased when you returned to your seat. When we were students at the university, one day we passed on Cass Avenue, and we stopped to say hello.

Cindy and Barbara, Ushers Club, *East Detroit High School Yearbook,* 1965.

MRS. MEYER

I wrote my first poem in your class. I was in 10th grade. We didn't read much poetry in school. At home there was only a Childcraft book of poems and a book by Longfellow. I read many of the books in the school library, but no poetry. You taught us how to write haiku, and the day after I brought my poem to class, you read it out loud. Something about a falling leaf. In autumn, I used to lie under the maple tree in our yard and watch the leaves fall. Probably something simple like—

> just a gentle breeze
> and the maple leaf breaks loose
> falling… fleeing… gone

Something indicating "gone" since I had not seen my mother for four years. Then "fleeing" because I counted the days until I could leave home. Eventually I did leave, and I became a poet, but I wrote my first poem in your class.

Marilyn Meyer. Grosse Pointe Farms, Mich.
B.A. DePauw University; M.A. Wayne State University. English.
East Detroit High School Yearbook, 1966.

LOUISA

Jo March, my favorite character of yours, was boyish and independent, a lot like you. As a young girl, I cried when her sister Beth died. You also lost your sister and you called her Beth. Rereading today, I cry again. When my mother was ill, she warned us of her coming death. We weren't quiet with our grief like Jo—instead, we wept and wailed. Not my father, though; he rarely shed a tear, stoic, surely frightened at his future alone with four children. Children should not have to experience death, so they say, and yet it's everywhere, a dog crushed by a truck, a dead bird, a grandfather in a casket, a tree struck by lightning, all those snowy days, the trees leafless, and then the next generation repopulates, we shut the book, wipe away the tears, do our homework and snuggle down under our blankets and fall asleep.

Louisa May Alcott. Photograph by James Norman, date created 1860-80. Courtesy of New York Public Library Berg Collection.

EILEEN

We used to skip school and sit in Henry's Drug Store, smoking together and talking about our missing parents, perhaps our boyfriends, our hair. You lived on Nine Mile Road in an old farmhouse still standing in a neighborhood of 1950 cinderblock houses. You weren't allowed guests. The shadowy figure of your grandmother would appear from behind the door watching you and calling your name, "Come inside, Eileen." You were slim, the lines in your face and body very noir. Long dark brown hair. Olive skin. Dark black eyeliner. You appeared in East Detroit High in the twelfth grade. You didn't do well in school. You smoked and worked at White Castle. I'd wait for you in front of your house and then we'd walk to school together. I saw you once after graduation. You were living with a guy, some secret there. The color orange comes to mind, maybe that was the color of the vinyl sofa in your apartment. The ceilings were low. The bedroom door was closed. It was dark. Sometime later, I invented an imaginary world in a novel, and you were at the center, intertwined with my double.

CATHERINE

As a young girl, I used to dream about you and the Moors, the craggy hills and storms, your losses reminding me of my own vulnerability to the winds of circumstance. Like me, your mother died early in life. Your stepbrother was motherless, too, neither of you loved as children. The love between you and he was like a return to the safety of the womb. "I *am* Heathcliff," you once said. "He's always, always in my mind… as my own being." Dying in childbirth, you left behind a daughter. For a while, she was subject to her uncle's cruelty, but eventually she boarded up that gloomy Wuthering Heights and married her cousin. A happy ending. What a relief. I used to plot my escape in my diary, imagining lovers and counting the days until I could leave. Meanwhile, I was lucky to have my sisters in the next room, and my brother downstairs. The Brontë children barely lived past thirty, but they relied on each other, too, for their survival.

Emily Brontë by Patrick Branwell Brontë, 1833.
Courtesy of National Portrait Gallery London.
Catherine Earnshaw is the main character in *Wuthering Heights*.

JANET

We took the bus together to and from school. A black coat wrapped around your thin body. We huddled in a corner in the attic in your rundown house a block away from mine, smoking your mother's cigarettes. "She drinks," you said, rolling your eyes. Little girls in every room. Your mother asleep on the couch. You bleached my hair platinum blonde to my father's dismay. Our favorite spot was the bowling alley. We drank coffee, ate French fries, and cussed out the waitress. How old are you girls? You gotta be eighteen to smoke in here. Your father would show up once in a while in a big car, wearing a fancy suit. He'd leave the girls a box of candy. The drive-ins. You're in the front seat with your boyfriend, Jim. I'm in the back with PZ. The lighted screen over the parking lot, catching it now and again from a horizontal position. At five to eleven, my father was waiting at the door with a list of questions about the movie. What could he do? Nothing. I was on my way out.

Janet and Barbara, 1966. Photo by Robert Henning.

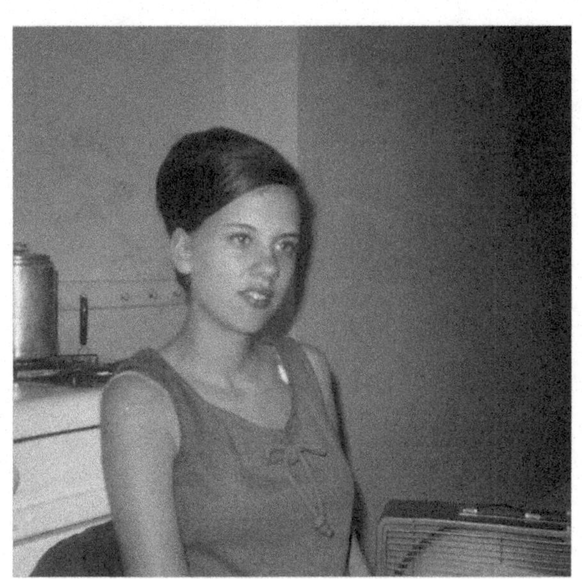

MARLENE

We didn't confide in each other. We weren't that close. We'd cruise the drive-ins in your red Mustang and go to parties together, searching for the boys we'd hook up with next. At a Christmas party in '66, I met a guy who I ran away with a few months later. Broke my father's heart, although back then, I wasn't quite sure he had one. After we children were gone and grown, he and my stepmother moved into a new house and bought a boat. One day you came along to watch him pull me over Lake St. Clair on water skis. I was treading water and holding my hand up to say stop, but he kept plowing forward—perhaps distracted by your curvy body in a bathing suit. He might have run me over, except in the nick of time, you tapped him on the shoulder. I still remember the look on your face when he cut the engine and swerved the boat around me.

Marlene, *East Detroit High School Yearbook,* 1966.

SHARON

I pulled my new car over to the curb in front of your house and honked. After you opened the door, you turned and waved to your mother standing on the porch. She was a short stout woman with big arms like my grandmother. We'd glide in and out of the drive-ins talking to boys. Your mother wasn't angry when you came home late. I imagined you talking to her about everything. Your life seemed safe to me. We didn't confide in each other, and yet there was something tender about you that I always liked. I trusted you. After I ran away from home, you had a job in a bank on Gratiot Avenue, and you'd pass phone money to my little sister so she could call me. Later you married your boyfriend and with a few days' notice, you were flown to Germany to stay with him while he was in the military. We wrote a few letters, but I couldn't find you after that because I didn't know your married name.

Sharon, *East Detroit High School Yearbook,* 1966.

KATHY

You used a big thick needle and a chunk of ice to pierce my ears. Close your eyes, you said, as you initiated me into womanhood. When I first met you, you were eighteen years old. Married at fourteen, you already had four children. Your husband was a construction worker, a close friend of the guy I was living with. They ordered us around. Get me a beer, do this, do that. A few years later, I was selling lemonade in a concession on the waterfront. Eerie Armenian music was broadcasting over the loudspeakers. The clouds were dark, threatening rain, and only a few people on the midway. Suddenly you appeared, walking along with a bag of books. You had just started college, you said, with a gleam in your eye. You were going to become a lawyer. You had left your husband, and your mother was watching the children.

Left: Kathy and Terry; right: Griffin and Barbara, 1967.

DONNA

For a while, we were roommates in an apartment on Manistique Street on the Eastside of Detroit. When you and your baby came home from the hospital, I was sleeping on the couch. Across the alley in my former apartment, my ex-boyfriend was sleeping with another girlfriend. You dressed up in a negligee and I took photos to send to your husband in Vietnam. Late into the night, we talked about your Jim and my new boyfriend just home from the Marines. Forget your ex, you said, get married and have a baby with the guy outside in his car waiting for you. I used to take care of your baby, but now I only remember a photograph with cereal on his face. I've tried to find you many times, but I only knew you by your husband's last name and his phone number long ago was disconnected. When we women marry again and again and keep moving further into the suburbs, finally we disappear.

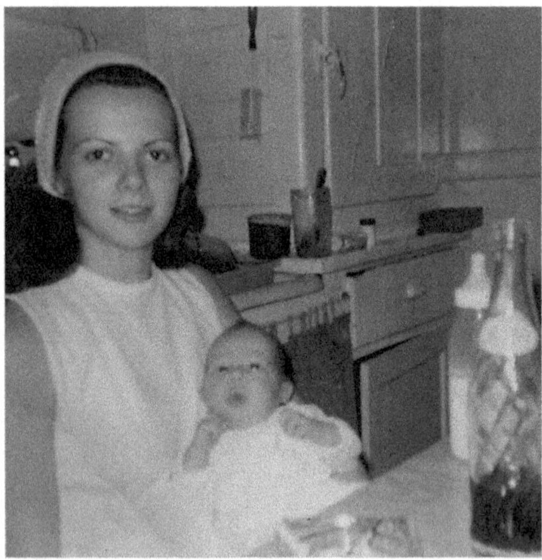

Donna, 1968. Photo by Barbara.

LINDA

I was working as a secretary in a data processing department at Chatham Supermarkets. You were working for a travel agency in Southfield. We were roommates in a flat in Madison Heights. You were reading about hypnosis. One day you asked me to sit on a stool while you tried to hypnotize me, swinging back and forth a rose birthstone on a chain. Your boyfriend was there, too. I was on the verge of tears. We went to a club with fake ID, and I had a panic attack. I never could handle alcohol. I crouched down on the floor in the back of the car. I remember telling you that your boyfriend couldn't be there all the time. There was only one bedroom. We must have lived together for a couple of months before you left with him, and I moved back into the city for a new job. When I look for you now on Facebook, lo and behold, you are a psychologist.

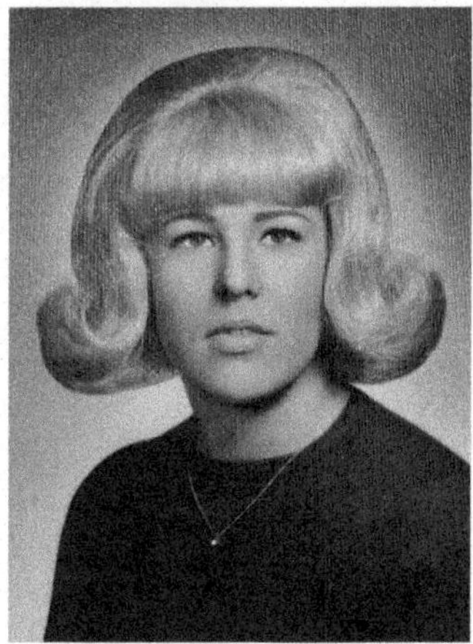

Linda Calder, 1967.

LUCY

You were tall, slim and black. We used to go out to lunch together. You worked in accounting at Faygo Pop and I was the secretary for the sales manager. You lived at home with your family, and I was sharing a flat with a roommate on Outer Drive. We both rode the bus to work. After I inherited my grandfather's old Dodge, sometimes I'd drop you off at home. I remember how you would slide down low in the seat so no one could see you as we drove through the neighborhoods. Sometimes instead of eating lunch, we'd go to Hudson's Department Store. Sometimes you show up in my dreams when I'm back in that office. We once imagined going on a trip together, down south where you had relatives, but this was '69 not long after Martin Luther King was assassinated, and we were afraid to drive out of the city in the same car together, but I remember we imagined it and then decided not to.

SUZIE

When you came to stay with me, I was living on Alter Road right down the street from where my mother had grown up. I remember you sitting on the sofa very pregnant, waiting. Your father had kicked you out of the house. Your brother was my boyfriend, and even though we were taking a break from each other, he asked me to help you out. I would come and go, to work and back, and there you'd be sitting on the sofa, looking out the window. I must have cooked for you. One day you left a note, saying you were on your way to the hospital. I went out with some friends from work to a bar in Hamtramck, and stupidly let a guy I met into the apartment. When I asked him to leave, he refused. He held me down with his hand on my throat and I lay there as still as possible. Afterwards, I pretended everything was normal. Did he want something to eat? After he left, I stood at the window in the dark and watched him drive away. The strange thing is—a fire had started in the house across the street. Flames were coming out of a window on the top floor. Moments later the fire department arrived. I stood there in the dark watching. A few days later, you came back to pick up your things. I didn't tell you about him. I didn't tell anyone. I was frightened he might return, and I was worried your brother would discover. I don't know where you are now or what happened to the baby. I moved on. We all moved on.

JEAN

After modeling for an art class in Old Main, I crossed the street to browse in Marwil's Bookstore. I liked the title and the photo on the cover, so I bought it. *Good Morning, Midnight.* A line from an Emily Dickinson poem. In her poem, everything comes around, the movement of the planet, even her desire for daylight as it passes through midnight into morning. For your character, Sasha, it's lights out, last call, even at noon, from one bar to another, one hotel room to another. No money, no friends. Nothing but the dark cavern of her consciousness. And you took us there. You grew up in the lush Caribbean, a middle child, without your mother's love, sent to school in England at seventeen. When family money dried up, you refused to return. Yes, sunshine was a sweet place, but you were in a city now working as a chorus girl, in love with a wealthy man. Money, love and gifts. Then he was gone. You say that sadness became part of you, so much so that you would have missed it, if gone, that melancholic cloud your women characters inhabit. In my late teens, after running away from home, I was tossed aside by my first lover, an older guy with many asides. I didn't turn to alcohol, like Sasha and you, but I was alone and deeply unhappy with visions of people and rooms from the past, ghostlike, continuing into the present. Later I wrote prose poems about a lost girl and a dark erotic novella about a woman working in a bar. The enticing dark side of the sun. Not a place to stay for long. Like you, I was lucky to be a writer and reader, and eventually I was lucky to learn how to breathe with my body and mind, in my own room, in rooms with others.

Jean Rhys, Montparnasse, 1921.

FAYE

You were seated on a stool and students were sprawled around the room, some at desks, some on the floor. You were silent for a few minutes. You had us write about a stone that you had placed on a table. Some of the students read what they had written. I was too shy to read out loud back then, and I was relieved you didn't call on me. The semester assignment, you said, was to choose an object we could carry around and write several poems about it. After class, I went directly to my counselor and dropped the class. Then I went to the bookstore to buy some of the books on your syllabus, including *Soap* by Francis Ponge and your book—*A Man Is a Hook. Trouble*—poems with fictional truth telling narrators and your surreal pointillism drawings, e.g, a man's headless body with penises erupting from every orifice. My friend Sally took classes, too, and she said you were one of the best teachers she ever had. The other day ago, in an on-line class, a student in Hawaii was talking about a teacher from whom he'd learned a lot about poetry, and it was you. You moved to Hawaii in 1980 and you're still there. For a while after your workshop, I carried an object, a bobby pin around with me and took notes in my journal. My mother used to snap pin curls into my hair with bobby pins. During World War II, a Detroit man road the buses, collecting unhinged hair pins and donating them for the war effort. A little thing can become a big thing. Even if we aren't aware of it.

Faye Kicknosway (aka Morgan Blair), 1974. Photo by Sally Young.

HARRIETTE

The day after the fire at Joni's, we both came to help her move, you with your van and me with our old car and trailer. I was eight months pregnant, and you asked if you could photograph me. Some hilarious photos, naked, like a pregnant witch, flying around the room on a broom. Then a difficult home birth. After two days of labor, we all went to the doctor's office in your van. Your water will break very soon, she said, so we hustled back home for a baby, my little girl, and you were there with your long hair, long legs, cowboy boots, and your 4 x 5 documenting every moment. You became a midwife photographer, and our families became close, so close that we became lovers for a short time, then friends who were once lovers. "Androgyny" was the word of our time, and we lived it. Once my toddler daughter pointed at a photograph on a Women's Studies textbook of a slim woman wearing a man's suit. She called out your name, "That's Harriette!" You were ten years older than me, the mother of three boys and several others who needed you. I loved the way you brought bits and pieces of the natural world into your house, into your photos. When I was living in Tucson, I sent you a devil's claw and you were ecstatic. Always struck by the messy wild world, its beauty, the excitement so much sometimes that you needed to calm down, chill out with a bottle of wine. One became two and for a long time, I didn't pick up the phone at night. In your late 70s, overnight you quit drinking and moved in with your son in Arizona on a ranch, near the border of Mexico. Even though the middle range of your eyesight is challenged, you still wake up in awe of the world, surrounded now by animals and desert plants.

Left: Harriette Hartigan and Barbara, Nov 17, 1975, photo by Allen Saperstein; middle: Harriette, 1980, photo by Barbara.

KATHY

Late at night, I find you sitting on the edge of the sofa in the dark listening to Van Morrison. You are usually a quiet person, kind of reserved, sometimes a little anxious, maybe more so this year after Jim's unexpected death. When I first met you, you were in med school, and you lived in a communal house two doors away from us. We had a dinner co-op on our block. Students, artists, writers, social activists. We were going to change things, live differently. When I became pregnant, you said you'd help with the birth. My other labor had lasted two days, and this baby was a month late. Gravity can help, I was told, so I kept pacing and singing about the saints marching in. While Allen helped me concentrate on my breathing, you caught the baby and helped the placenta release. Then you had to go back to school. Word was out that a med student was helping someone with a home delivery, and that wasn't allowed back then. Today, I am upstairs in your house preparing for a reading and you're downstairs in your office, humming and singing in preparation for tomorrow's choir practice. Out front the trees are swaying in the wind. In the back, a flock of blue jays mingles with the squirrels for the seeds you scatter. I remember just eight months ago, walking along with you, Jim and the geese on the lawns at the Ford mansion, now a museum and public park. Jim was quiet and gentle. I didn't know him in the '70s.

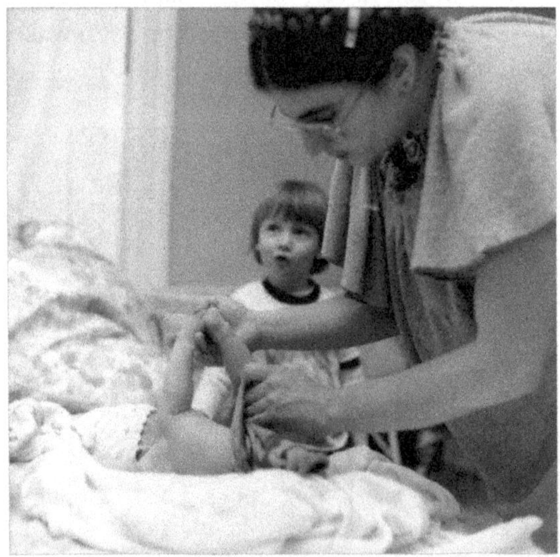

Newborn Michah, Linnée and Kathy Fulgenzi, Feb. 23, 1979.
Photo by Harriette Hartigan.

ANNE

You were my daughter's first babysitter. After graduating from high school, you backpacked through Europe on your own. I gave you my juicer in trade for babysitting. Soon we were both adults and we would dance and drink at Alvin's until we were sweaty. When you were on break from college, we took a train to New Orleans for the Jazz Fest with the guys in your boyfriend's band. All of us slept together on the floor in your small apartment. When your mother took your little brother and disappeared on the back roads out west, you couldn't find her and after a while you stopped trying. I would talk about my mother all the time, but your way of coping was to keep it all to yourself. When I finally made the move to New York in my father's old station wagon, you came along for the ride. Then you helped Allen take care of the children until he could make the trip. Years later, when I moved to Tucson, we lived a few blocks apart. I remember walking past the orange trees, with you and your two big golden dogs. After your knee surgery, I helped you wash your hair, bathe and do physical therapy. Now you visit me in Brooklyn and sleep on a mat on my floor. Once when I said I was in love with someone, you smiled and said, "Barbara, I have no idea what you're talking about. I have had only two boyfriends in my life, and I married them both."

Left: Anne Urban making funnel cakes, 1976, photo by Barbara; right: Michah, Barbara, Linnée and Anne 1983, photo by Allen Saperstein.

MARIANNE

You and my brother were a couple. You made feather earrings and sold them on the street and at the Ann Arbor Art Fair. Allen and I were selling popcorn and caramel apples. Then at night we curled up with our children, some of us in our van and some of us in sleeping bags, on a lawn near the university. When my daughter was a baby, you'd bring your two little boys over to my house. They'd run around the apartment and make Linnée laugh. Then you met someone else, got pregnant, and after the baby was born you joined the Hari Krishnas. You took your children and headed somewhere down South, without telling anyone where you were going, perhaps running from your first husband, the boys' father. I've searched for you online many times. When I ask around to other friends in Detroit who once knew you, no one has heard a word.

Marianne at the Ann Arbor Art Fair, 1976. Photo by Barbara.

HALIMA

In the early '70s, you, Allen and I set off on a journey to festivals and carnivals in Michigan and down south. We led the caravan with our Ford Galaxy and trailer, and you followed in an old rusty Karmann Ghia. We slept together in rooms, tents and cars. We put our tiny bits of cash together to eat. From the Detroit State Fair to Hillsdale, Michigan to Birmingham, Alabama, you sold astrology charts and read palms and, with an old box camera, we took photos of people dressed in antique clothing. I remember you and Allen drinking vodka together and carrying on laughing and telling stories. After your daughter graduated from high school, we drove you to New York so you could marry Mac. You had worked long hours to raise her, mostly as a waitress. In New York, you studied English literature, went to law school, and finally practiced law with your husband. You moved from a rented flat on the Eastside of Detroit to an apartment in Forest Hills to a house in Seacliff near the Hempstead Bay. When Allen was ill, you came into Brooklyn, climbed the four flights to his apartment, to say goodbye to him. After you died, Mac told me you kept drinking and smoking to the end, and he said you had suffered from deep sadness and a difficult childhood. Your birthdate was the same as my mother's, November 4th, my mother in '21, you in '39. You watched me leave Allen, take a lover, pack up the kids and move to New York City. You once gave me a warning, "Like your mother and me, you are a Scorpio. Be careful of drama, Barbara. Don't make decisions too quickly."

Left: Halima and Linnée, 1976; right: Halima, Dec. 24, 1979. Photos by Barbara.

BERNADETTE

We once took a trip together to New York in my old Honda, the radio on the blink, but we had a tape recorder with us, and we shared earplugs, one for you and one for me. On the way home, as we passed through the Pennsylvania mountains and over the Ohio fields, on some back road we saw a man with felt paintings for sale, several propped up against his car. I made some comment and then we argued—you said a felt painting could never be art. It got hot and close in the car with no way out. A slap on the knee. Was it you or me? I don't remember. And neither do you. Later you hooked up with Allen's best friend Joe, and you two married, moved up north, then a breakup, then reunited, but Joe died from a heart attack just days before he planned to come back home. A few months earlier, when he was in New York, he phoned me. He wanted to meet and talk. But I was helping you, and you were so unhappy that I didn't want to get in the middle. So I declined. I was kind to him, I think, but I didn't expect him to die. I had known him for years, and loved him. I flew to Detroit and helped you pack up his painting studio. Once on my way up north to visit with my sister, I stopped in Traverse City and we had dinner. You were retired from the library and involved with a theater group. Even though years have passed since I last saw you, this morning, I woke up thinking about you and that silly argument.

Bernadette Groppuso and Michah, 1983. Photo by Allen Saperstein.

ESTHER

You had a gig at Sarah Lawrence College in New York, and you asked me to sub for your Wayne State class in trade for helping me with the stories I was writing. When you walked into the room, you were on stage, inspirational, the students clearly in awe of you, an author, professor and a sexy mother with five grown children. I was reading your book, *Her Mothers*, when I went into labor with my second child. You open with a quote from Virginia Woolf: "A woman writing thinks back through her mothers." Your character Beatrix searches through her historical and literary mothers, and in the end, her daughter—on her own search—finds Beatrix. You came to our house for the birth of our son, but you had to rush back to campus for a class. When you returned, Michah was already with us. A few weeks later, Phyllis Chesler read at your apartment from her book about mothering. While listening and nursing my baby, I realized—it sounds odd to say this now, but I wasn't conscious until that moment that I'd been editing out domestic narratives and details as if they weren't important. We both moved to New York, and you invited me to a feminist seder. Right from the beginning, I was in awe and in love with you. In '89 in Cincinnati, after giving the graduation speech at Union Institute, you gave me a small hand painted metal turtle. It still sits on the shelf above my desk. When reading from my novel, *You, Me and the Insects* at Mid-Manhattan Library, I looked up, and there you were in the audience, my teacher and mentor. You whispered as you hugged me goodbye, "Good luck, Dear." Like my mother, you always called me "Dear."

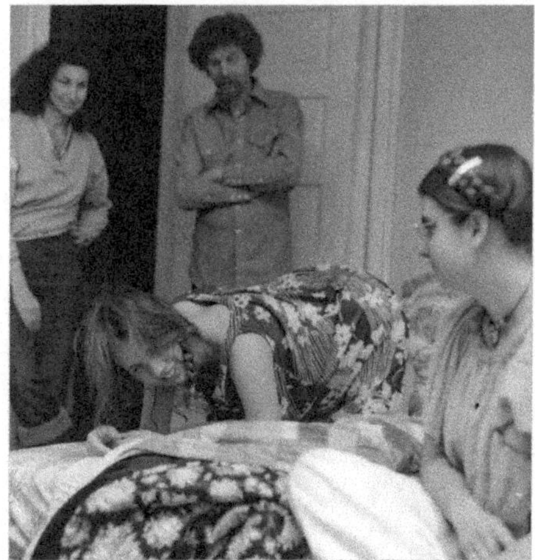

Left: Barbara and Esther Broner in Cincinnati, 1988; right: Esther, Allen, Barbara and Kathy Fulgenzi at Michah's birth, Feb 23, 1979, photo by Harriette Hartigan.

NANCY

I used to bring my four-year-old daughter to class with me. She'd sit quietly beside me and draw while you lectured and led discussions about 19th century novels. When I stopped by your office to talk about the paper I was writing, you gave me your home phone number just in case I had any questions. I was writing on *Jane Eyre* and *Hard Times.* I remember working in the typing room in the library and going downstairs to the phone booth to call you. I'd read a few sentences, and you'd comment or ask another question, then back to the typewriter. In a very supportive letter, recommending me for grad school, you mentioned my paper was about marriage, about power, inheritance rights, the laboring class, and the educational system, surely many of the points you had lectured on. At the time, I was absorbed with my own marriage and family problems; with two children and not much cash, I needed to figure out how to separate from my children's father. No wonder I was writing about marriage. I remember once speaking to you about my concern that pursuing a graduate degree was a selfish endeavor, not useful to society. You reminded me that my happiness was beneficial to society. You must have also talked about teaching and the history of ideas. A few years after our class, you published a book, with much acclaim, *Desire and Domestic Fiction: A Political History of the Novel.* Maybe I never would have applied to Wayne State's grad school in English if you had not encouraged me. In that case, I might never have become a teacher for the many students who I later encouraged. Lines of energy would have re-formed and rearranged in a completely different pattern.

Nancy Armstrong, 1977.

VIRGINIA

You explain in a piece written for the Memoir Club that as you tried to release your obsession with your mother, your novel, *To the Lighthouse* came to you in a rush. I felt an affinity with you; we both had lost our mothers in childhood and both from rheumatic fever. For a graduate school party, I once scoured the resales to dress up like you. Your novel was one of the most beautiful and lyrical I'd ever read; the thinking mind of one character flows into another with the very slight distance of a narrator who knows precisely what each is thinking, our shared consciousness one field, held together, readers and characters. Maybe it was difficult to always be attuned to the voices and minds of others. Maybe after the family losses, the war, these voices came louder and darker, maybe you put stones in your pockets and walked into the river to free yourself from the voices that made your writing so beautiful. In your memoir, you said you could not write of the depths of the past unless the present was smooth. With peace, you could tell the story—"Let me then like a child advancing with bare feet into a cold river, descend again into that stream." I wasn't thinking of you when I wrote about my mother, but your book and your voice were part of my memory. After Mrs. Ramsay dies and the war is over, we readers flow out on the sea in a boat heading to the lighthouse with Mr. Ramsay, and his children, Cam and James, who now, without realizing it, carry along the stream of their familial consciousness.

Left: Barbara as Virginia Woolf, 1982; right: Lytton Strachey and Virginia Woolf at Garsington Manor, 1923, photo by Lady Ottoline Morrell. Courtesy of National Portrait Gallery, London.

NORMA

You were intellectual, a history buff. You didn't like to gossip. You always wore jeans and a tee shirt. Your face would often break into an easy wide laugh, especially around children. When our toddlers became friends at nursery school, we used to take turns with playdates and babysitting. We were part of a group of mothers who hung out together with our children. There were picnics and roller-skating parties. Many afternoons, we sat in my kitchen drinking coffee and watching our children play in the sandbox. You were working at Wayne State bookstore. I was in grad school. You had your second baby in a birthing center, and I came along to help take care of Jamie. After the children were a little older, you took a job delivering mail on the southwest side where you had grown up. Your father worked for the post office, and how easy it was for you to stop at a bar on breaks, you said, lunch hours and after work. Then more and more. Not long after, you and your husband divorced, and Al and I split up. For a while you were staying in a hotel on Cass Avenue. Some years back when you visited me in New York, we had dinner together at an Italian place in the East Village. Then my emails were returned and phone numbers disconnected. After paying for a people search, *voila,* we are reconnected and there you are on FB surrounded by—I count six—grandchildren.

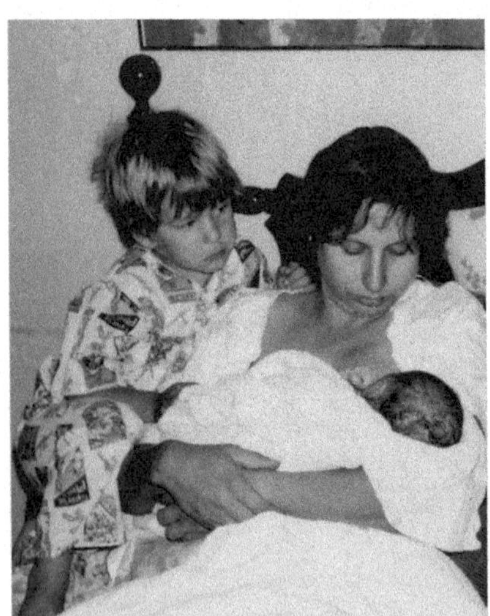

Left: Jamie, Norma Bliss Cook and Daniel, 1980, photo by Barbara; right: Barb and Norma, 2003.

SALLY

In '72, I'd sit at the bar in Cobbs with my book and my short beer, and I'd watch you and Allen bartending. Married to the drummer in Shadowfax, you became pregnant shortly after me. You cooked for our toddlers in Monteith Nursery, and every day you prepared and pulled their lunch and snacks to school in a wagon, along with your little girl, Esther. You babysat for Michah when he was only a few days old, so we could spend time with Linnée. After Allen and I broke up, and I was feeling low, you came over and cleaned my apartment. In the early '80s, you moved to the East Village, living in a third-floor walkup floor-thru apartment, with a police lock on the door and an extra mattress in the hallway room. I stayed with you for a few weeks while looking for a job. You helped me turn an old Brooklyn tire shop into Allen's copy center, painting and building walls, a sleeping loft and counters. The ceiling is still the dark green we painted it, although now it's an Italian grocery. With endless creative energy, you made art—abstract city paintings, inside and out, collages, toy soldiers on old turntables and so on. You built stage scenery, designed clothes and hats, sold them in the street markets, opened a store, worked in the schools, taught children how to sew and make art, and planted vegetables and ran events in the Avenue B garden, and more. You were the art editor for the first issue of *Long News,* your collages in all five issues. For years, every Thanksgiving, I'd head over to your place for a potluck. On my fridge, there's a button I bought at Santo's, made by you. Whenever I open the fridge, I think of you: Welcome to McHattan.

Left: Barbara and Sally Young at KGB Bar, 2005, photo by Cliff Fyman; right: Barb, Sally and Raken Leaves, 1984.

GRACE

On the first day of a class on 20th Century American Lit, the male teacher handed us the syllabus. There were too many books," he said, and he suggested cutting, *Enormous Changes at the Last Minute.* I looked around and raised my hand. "But there are only two women on the syllabus. Can't we eliminate one of the men?" I don't remember which book he dropped, but it wasn't yours. Not long after, you came to the Detroit Institute of Arts to give a reading. You were about sixty years old, wearing jeans, chewing gum and popping bubbles. When someone asked why you didn't write more, you just smiled and said, "Art is long, but life is too short." Your character Faith and her friends were social activists (like you). My generation was the age of your children, and we were also reinventing family to include friends, live-in lovers, sometimes with communal living. You write in the introduction to your collected, "As a grown woman, I had no choice. Everyday life, kitchen life, children life had been handed to me, my portion, the beginning of big luck, though I didn't know it." Into your stories you channeled the voices of friends and neighbors in your kitchens, on the stoops and in the playgrounds. Nothing flat or monologic, no static voice, very open ended, the world and consciousness alive and continually changing. In one of your early stories, Faith's little boy, Tonto, talks her into holding his feet while he yells something *so important* out the window of their third floor apartment to his older brother—he yells, "Richie, hey, Richie!… I'm playing with your new birthday-present army fort and all them men." He slams the window shut and says, "I bet he's mad!" I remember leaning out a window in our Brooklyn apartment as my son and his friend raced down the street after tearing a hole in a wall I had just repaired, and I yelled, "I hate boys!" Did I really hate them? Not hardly. Maybe a little too permissive, but like Faith and perhaps you, too, I always had his back.

Grace Paley, courtesy of The New York Public Library. Digital Collections. 1960–1961.

KAREN

Your grown daughter's face carries a slight imprint of yours, but her body's strong, her movements confident. As I glance into the living room, my eyes stop at a couch with a blanket. I ask her if she knows what happened here. "Everyone else was upstairs, sleeping, but Karen was down here on the couch," she says. "The door was unlocked, and the man came in." "He raped her," I add. Your child begins to cry, "She never told me that. She never said so." "Maybe I'm wrong. I do that sometimes, collapse my own experience with another," I say. But at night when I close my eyes, I hear your voice telling me—*he put a pillow over my face, he hurt me.* One of the last times I saw you, someone snapped a photo of us in Alvin's, standing under the Twilight Bar sign. I can still hear your deep throaty laugh. I remember your house, the spectacular vegetable garden, the tree swing, all the children you watched, mine included. We used to imagine living together in old age in a communal house, but I was in New York, you in Detroit and as the years passed, we stopped calling. As I drive away from the house where you lived, Aretha's on the car radio singing about a tiny sparrow, "Come now all you fair and tender maidens." In my mind's eye, your willowy body is like a star on a summer morn, and you're in your yard sitting under that old cherry tree, surrounded by a group of little children who loved you, and you loved them, too—

Left: Karen Fostey Lemming, two other children, and Karen's son Nathan, 1979, photo by Barbara; right: Barbara and Karen, in Alvin's, 1989.

KAY

You and Mike were the supers in our building in the Cass Corridor, and all three of us were poets. You were a young woman from cornfield Minnesota. In *Poetry Detroit,* I find a couple of your poems from the '70s, both expressing a need for silence and a spiritual connection with the earth. In late night phone calls, you'd listen to my new poems. One day after I threw my manuscript in the garbage bin out in the alley, you convinced me to go back for it. While digging around, I found a bag of antique women's clothing. In a swishy dress, I coaxed you to leave your baby with Mike and go out with me to Alvin's. We liked the sound of the words when ordering—Give me a scotch on the rocks—but in fact neither of us were drinkers, both easily tipsy. We flirted with some friends at the bar, like the characters in my poems—that night I was tough Lorraine and you were the vulnerable ghost girl out on the town. A guy I was seeing walked us home, and you remind me in a recent phone conversation that we stood out front of our building taking turns kissing him. We were happy to get home safe. A few days later, I turned off the bath and went back to the typewriter in my bedroom to change a word in a poem. A man was standing in the middle of the room. I pivoted, crumpled up the poem and ran. He chased me out of the apartment, locking the door behind me. "My children." Half dressed, I pounded and screamed. Neighbors came, you and Mike came, a body builder from another apartment broke down the door. Miraculously, the children were still asleep, and he had gone back out the window. The next day, you helped us move upstairs. Not long after that, I moved to New York and you moved to Romeo, north of Detroit, a small town for a small-town girl.

Kay Johnson Maniscalco and Molly, Dallie in the Alley, 1979.

H.D.

You were almost six feet tall and very elegant. Your first boyfriend, Ezra Pound, named you H.D., but sometimes he also called you Saint Hilda. You travelled to Vienna for analysis with Freud, and he helped you recover from a nervous breakdown, war terrors, writer's block and discomfort with your bi-sexuality. You called him Papa. In '81, my professor, Charlie Baxter, suggested I read your epic poem, *Trilogy*. At the time, I was a bit skeptical about the religious figures. Even though I was raised Christian, and my mother had visions of Jesus calling her when she was ill, I regarded religion as an illusion, maybe necessary for some, but not for me. But your figures were not exactly religious; instead, they were part of your personal mythology, along with the Greeks and Egyptians. The poet Barbara Guest explains in your biography that the angels and religious figures "were always present in an unconscious nourished from childhood on Moravian history and doctrines." The Moravians were a small pacifist protestant sect who had settled in Bethlehem, Pennsylvania where you grew up. I can't help but wonder if these figures wandering around in your unconscious also may have contributed to your nervous breakdowns. After living through two horrifying wars, in *Trilogy* you make a plea for peace and for the scribes, the poets, to be recognized, to prophesize, to learn from the ancients. After all, destruction from war wasn't new, it had happened before. And it will happen again. The lady comes, carrying a blank book. Isn't that your book? Isn't that you? The lines of the poem slowly emerge on the pages—like a palimpsest—gods, goddesses, angels, wisemen and the women around Jesus meld one into another, like a dream, as you call forth with your word-alchemy the feminine principle, to create anew with wisdom and love the creation continual, and this knowledge is passed along through the ages, by scribes, artists, magicians and by you, to all of us, the poet's dharma—*a half-burnt-out apple-tree / blossoming*

Hilda Doolittle, 1900–1922, n.d., courtesy of the Beinecke Rare Book & Manuscript Library.

JOAN

You rarely told me anything about yourself. I gathered from a comment here and there that you were Catholic, you were athletic, and you liked to sail. When I went to see you the first time, you asked what I was feeling, and I replied, *What do you mean? Could you give me an example?* Then I tried this new way of communicating on my father. "I feel angry when you..." "What do you mean you're angry?" he snarled. I remember lying under an elm tree outside your office, staring up at the leaves and feeling incompetent with my life. Allen and I had split up and soon we were moving to New York, together and apart. You were also moving within weeks to Miami with a girlfriend. After a while we talked over the phone, then a few letters. Forty years later, I found a phone number. You were surprised to hear from me. I thanked you for helping me as a young woman. Your voice sounded weak. You told me how you had taken care of your dying husband and then your mother and father. After your father's funeral, you were standing on the sidewalk when suddenly you felt a terrible pain in your back. You woke up in a hospital. An 18-wheeler with no side-mirrors or backup signals had backed up onto the sidewalk, hitting you and pinning you under the truck, breaking several bones. You talked about online classes you were taking in theology. You were happy to hear from me. I thanked you again. You always wanted to help others, you said. Stunned at the amount of suffering you must have endured, I tried to console you.

Michah waiting at the car; Joan and Linnée, 1983.
Photo by Barbara.

MARGUERITE

As we walked along Canal Street, my poet-lover carried *The Lover* in the pocket of his long black coat. You'll like this book, he said. It wasn't a gift. It had to be returned. On the cover, a stain where he'd once set a coffee cup over your eye. After returning the book, I bought my own copy and made an identical coffee stain. A disturbing and seductive coming of age story. Autobiography and fiction intertwined. Your story, but not your story. A child on her way to school in a silk dress, high heels and a man's floppy hat. A fifteen-year-old girl with an abusive brother, a mentally challenged younger brother and an unstable sometimes violent mother. And all three of you "loved her beyond love." To write straight out narrative would have captured the desire and clipped it short. I learned a lot about writing novels from studying your books—the indirectness, the shifting of time and point of view, the circling around images and looping back with memories of the scene at the ferry—the face, your face, the hat, your hat, the river, the debris, the muddy light. Each page a poem. Upon observing the mother mentally drifting away from her, you and your narrator explain: "I went mad in full possession of my senses. Just long enough to cry out. I did cry out. A faint cry, a call for help, to crack the ice in which the whole scene was fatally freezing. My mother turned her head." The ship heads away from the shore, the lover's black car disappearing as you travel across the China Sea, the Red Sea, the Indian Ocean, the Suez Canal, landing in France where you live the rest of your life.

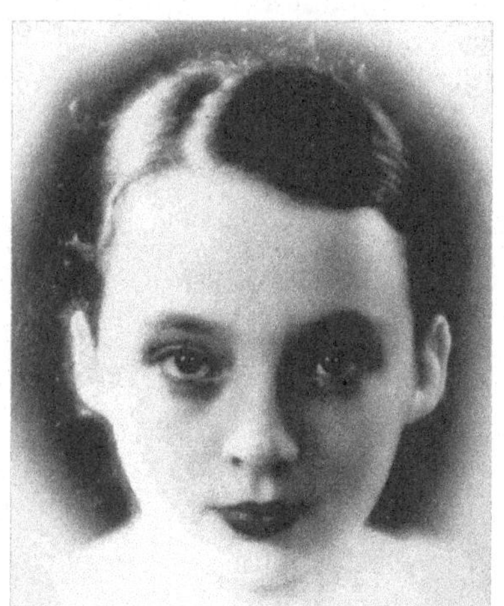

Left: Marguerite Duras, 1930; right: 1974, photo by Edouard Boubat.

MARY

When you left your neighborhood for the first time, as a child, you were surprised to discover that not everyone spoke with an Irish brogue. Both your parents had immigrated to New York from Ireland. After attending an all-girl Catholic high school, you became a Dominican nun, for fifteen years living in a convent and teaching Greek and Latin in Catholic schools in East New York. Your first lover was a young man who left the priesthood for political reasons. You left because the Church wasn't serving those who needed the most help. You were active in Vietnam anti-War protests and in the Civil Rights Movement. As a professor, you helped young women—with little or no experience outside their families and neighborhoods—learn how to teach in Brownsville, one of the poorest neighborhoods in New York. You were the core faculty on my Ph.D. committee, and you talked to me almost every night when during a tenure review, I was attacked for having attended a non-traditional program. I remember visiting with you in the Catskills, the walks we took in the forest. Your life with your husband was calm and quiet, not like my up and down bohemian family life in Brooklyn. Even though we were a generation apart and lived utterly different lives, we liked to visit museums, see films and talk about books. You're ninety years old now and still living in the Catskills. Your husband died, but you have friends and a young man takes you to the supermarket twice a week. On the phone, you talk excitedly about a film you saw recently, *The Quiet Girl,* Claire Keegan's story about a neglected Irish girl. You remind me that you had a very happy childhood.

Mary Sheerin and Barbara, Taos, 1991.

LUANNE

You were a therapist married to a psychiatrist. You were reading Lacan and writing about your patients in your dissertation, patients with difficult mental patterns. At the time, I was in a Lacanian reading group. Your writing was experimental, almost literary. There was a way your mind joined the minds of your patients, and I found that interesting. You asked me to be on your Ph.D. committee and the first meeting was held in Taos. I loved New Mexico. Several times, you came to New York and I visited you in Taos. Once you took me into the desert to meet Louise Bourgeoise's son, Jean Louis. He was living off grid with no public services, no address, no taxes. I remember the fields of sage surrounding his house. I fantasized about living like that. Several years later I did live in New Mexico for a year, but not off-grid. I remember you didn't like my boyfriend, a philosopher who never arrived on time for appointments, sometimes an hour or two late. He drove me crazy. I watched you flirt with him, well maybe it wasn't flirting, but it seemed like it at the time. You both had a tendency to sexualize your gestures and expressions, maybe for you the result of childhood trauma. Then you insisted on not revising your dissertation, essentially pitting me against the head of your committee, who was also a friend of mine. Why was it so difficult to follow guidelines that you had created? Maybe it had something to do with the fact that, as young women, Mary was a nun and you were a sex worker. The last time I stayed at your place, I felt as if I couldn't breathe. I remember you standing behind a door, listening as I made a phone call. I was trying to change my plane ticket to go home sooner. After that, I stopped seeing you. Now I ask myself a question a therapist once put to me—What part did I play in that which I bemoan? Even now, I'm not sure.

MARIE

We lived on the same block on 9th Street and our boys went back and forth between our apartments, looking for a place with no parent around. We were always on alert to put a stop to some of their plans—dropping water balloons off the roof on passersby, throwing vegetables into the neighbor's yard in the middle of the night and so on. We were both strapped with big student loans. Once we had a meeting in your apartment about forming a coalition to fight for student loan forgiveness. We put an ad in the newspaper, but for some reason, we never followed through. I remember riding our bikes south on Ocean Parkway, heading to your aunt's house in South Brooklyn where you had grown up, but I got a flat tire and we had to walk our bikes back. You came to some of my poetry readings, even though poetry wasn't your thing. Once you made a presentation to a class I was teaching; we were reading Foucault's *Discipline and Punish*, and you talked about the prisons in New York, how crowded and hopeless the situation was for the inmates. We celebrated the children's birthdays together. The one I remember most is Linnée's 16th. She didn't want a party, but I made a cake for her. You and Armando came over, Allen and Michah were there, too. But Linnée refused to come out of her room. We stood at her closed bedroom door holding the cake and singing to her. It was hilarious. Then the kids got older. "That went by so fast," you said last night on the phone. Eventually, I turned our 9th Street apartment over to Allen, and you left your job in Criminal Defense at Legal Aid and moved to New Orleans to defend people on death row.

Marie Scavetta and Barbara at Marie's apartment on 9th Street, 1994.

MINA

A beautiful and flamboyant woman, writing experimental feminist poems, passionate free verse, a poetry of ideas, purposely tripping up the reader with a complex vocabulary. A mother, a poet and a visual artist. An artist-entrepreneur, designing and selling lampshades, hats and clothing in Paris and New York City. An eccentric old woman living on the Bowery, making poems and art with and about the homeless men who wandered the streets. Throughout your life, whatever you saw as unfair, you actively resisted. In an agreed upon marriage of convenience with Stephen Haweis, you escaped parental control. Sometimes under his thumb, sometimes free. After a brief collaboration with the Futurists—"Marinetti influenced me," you said, "merely by waking me up"—you moved to New York, got a divorce and followed Arthur Craven, a poet-boxer to Mexico. You lived there, rough, like hippies in the '60s and '70s. After he disappeared at sea and after three years away from your children, you returned to Europe, pregnant and grief-stricken, only to discover that Stephen had taken your son, Giles, to live with him in the Caribbean. Over and over, you left your children with this nurse or that school. When Giles came down with a rare form of cancer, he died, wondering why you refused to answer his letters and why your dislike for his father had affected your love for him. At night while reading your biography, I wept for Giles. Surely I was collapsing his situation with my own—for the long ago loss of my young mother. Maybe you thought your children were better off with the nurse. Back then, we didn't think about childhood like we do now. If only you had left behind letters and journals, then I might understand. After you moved to Colorado, a young writer, Martie Sterling, came to visit and you told her you were lonely, but your daughters (who had always supported you) were busy. Then you added, "But why should I expect them to spend so much time with me when I spent so little time with them?"

Mina Loy with daughter Oda (c. 1904, d. 1905).

DEBORAH

You were a political activist, as was your older sister and both your parents, your father, a lawyer who did lots of pro bono work. My parents had barely graduated from high school, their politics predictable. I went to DC with you for a few protests, once with my daughter, for women's right to abortion. Once, while camping along the Pacific, we sat around a campfire with your brother, and you two sang "Sgt. Pepper's Lonely Hearts Club Band." We went to dances to support leftist causes in Latin America. For a while, I was obsessed with reading everything by Mikhail Bakhtin, and I gave you a copy of *The Dialogic Imagination.* I went to your father's funeral, I was a witness at the County Clerk's Office for your wedding, and afterwards you handed me your new book about teaching. Today I reread the chapter you wrote about me and one of my students (with pseudonyms), my identity thinly veiled. In an interview, I talked openly, laid back, home talk, friend talk, about my parents, my students, my teaching. I never expected you to psychoanalyze me, to quote my working-class slang and to include details about my family. Sometimes say less, my mother suggested to me more than once. Later you apologized and said you'd never again use friends or co-workers as research subjects. You didn't intend to hurt me, but the problem with books is they tend to stick around. Today, a warm cloudy day in November, we sit outside Café Coulour. You tell me news of your life and I tell you mine. I had planned to talk to you about the book and how I feel about it. But 25 years ago? Your face is tense, your body more fragile with age. The sun emerges from a cloud cover. "Why don't they put up the awning?" I ask. What good would it do to bring it up now? I don't want to cause harm or stress. In fact, I'm very fond of you, sometimes I even forget about the book. Give Linnée and Michah and Esther my love," you say. And I do.

Deborah Mutnick and Barbara, Berkley, CA, 1987.

JULIA

I once taught a class on American lit and melancholia and I included your book, *Black Sun: Depression and Melancholia.* When I gazed at the black and white print of Holbein's painting of Christ in the tomb, it was as if I was standing at my mother's bedside looking at her body. Jesus, she told me, had appeared in the hospital, calling for her. Here he is flat-out dead, cast aside, mortal. Holbein must have suffered to paint him like this—Father, why have you abandoned me? I'd been mourning my mother for years. You are going in circles, my therapist said, our analysis is not working. Well, if I'm going to suffer like this, I thought, I might as well enjoy it. I wrote a novella, *Black Lace,* about a young woman whose parents had abandoned her and how, as an adult, she tried to free herself from identifying as a victim. Some years later when it was published, I opened the novella with a passage from your book: "*Melancholia* belongs in the celestial realm. It changes darkness into redness or into a sun that remains black, to be sure, but is nevertheless the sun, source of dazzling light." I wanted to give the reader a hint of light. Perhaps you did, too, after all, you are an analyst who believes in the possibility of change. By then I'd already snapped out of my intermittent love affair with loss. How? Not through analysis, at least not directly. When I started practicing yoga, the breath work and movement pulled my mind back into my body. A reminder, a tattoo I wanted, but never endured: *My body is my home.* For some reason, I found that idea incredibly freeing.

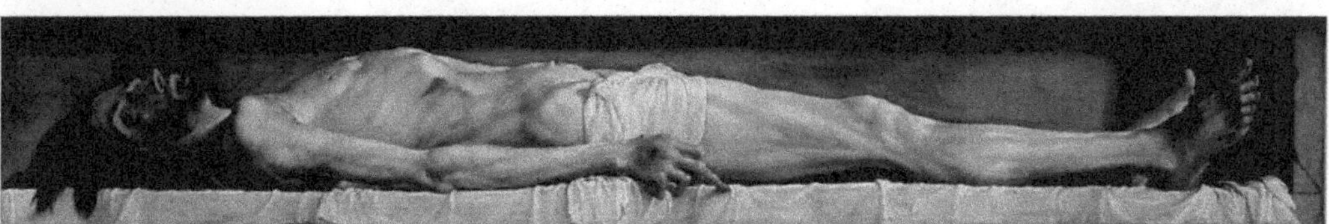

Left: Julia Kristeva, *Interviews,* trans. Ross Mitchell Guberman, Columbia University Press, 1996; right: Hans Holbein the Younger's "The Body of the Dead Christ in the Tomb" (1520–1522).

ANELE

In the morning, I'd stand in the doorway of your building, waiting for you. Once I was wearing two different colored socks and you ran back upstairs to find a matching pair for me. Walking down 5th Avenue to Flatbush to Dekalb to LIU, we shared our worries about our children. Why was she staying with her friend's family so much? Was it the back and forth between Allen and me? Were we too unconventional? Sometimes we cried together. We defended our children. Was it the awful gym teacher who chased him up the stairs yelling, I'll rip your face off, or the week in the basement for tapping a pencil. And he wasn't tapping. Or was he— When I think of you, it's these walks and talks that come to mind. You'd tell a story about one of your sisters or about growing up in Louisiana, then I'd segue in with a story about one of mine or something about politics or poetry or friends or dangerous encounters, whatever the topic—we were poets, both talkers and storytellers. On the way home, we'd sometimes take a break and stop at the Dominican restaurant for a pineapple juice. Sometimes, I'd run into you in the laundromat or on the street or in Copy Cat where you were chatting with Allen. After our children were grown, I moved out of town for a few years, and then you and Eric moved, too. Sometimes we reconnect with a phone call. Yesterday we talked—one story after another—while you were on your porch in Rhinebeck—a breeze, you said—and I was in my apartment in Brooklyn, the air conditioner running.

Left: Anele Rubin, 1989, photo by Eric Banks; right: David and Anele, photo by Madeline Rubin.

GEORGIA

In the middle of the cavernous Catskills, we took off our clothes and hopped around on the stones in the river, taking photos of each other, reclining, standing, and you made the photos into two collages, each like a hand of cards. You carefully removed a fanshaped mushroom from a tree in the forest, then etched a tiny tree branch on its side, and gave it to me. At the art colony you were studying the sky, drawing treetops on white folded Japanese paper and, under the wild trees and in the wind while watching you draw, I wrote a series of collaged sonnets. Everyday we escaped down the road to an open air aikido dojo where we learned how to fall down, roll over and stand up. In Provincetown, I stayed with you at your cottage, showered on the porch, swam and walked along the shore. I remember sitting on the beach reading *Moby Dick* and taking notes for a long poem I would later write. When Allen died, I came to you in grief. When you were in the hospital for a surgery, I helped you shower and wash your hair. I always loved sharing your relationship with space. Even the table setting brought a sense of quiet and peace, a way of distracting from the losses we encounter in life. I watched you working day by day in your studio and I brought some of your discipline and sensibility into my own life and art. After you married, you were often in Rhode Island and Paris, I was in India and out west, and we rarely saw each other, but I remember once sitting with you outside Café Orlin while we watched the pouring rain gush over the awning onto the sidewalk and street.

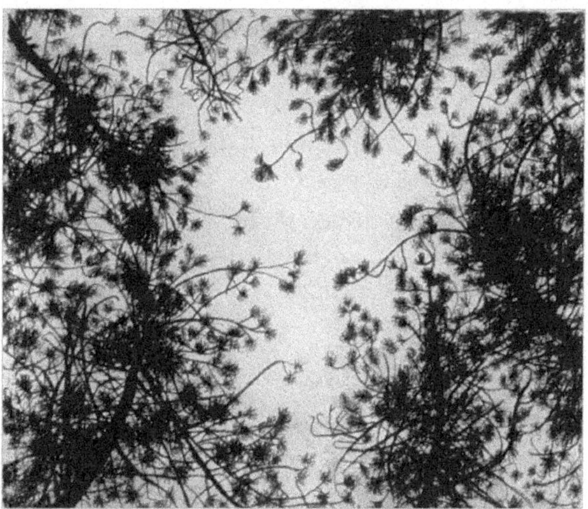

Left: Georgia Marsh and Barbara, Provincetown, 1994; right: Georgia's "Cooper Lake," 24x18, 1992, charcoal on handmade paper.

ELSA

You lost your mother when you were a teenager. Your father put her in a sanatorium, and she died of cancer in 1893. Thirty years later, you wrote a letter to Mary Reynolds Fitzgerald, "I love her now—in me—I am she—I have her message! I have to fill her shape—full—fill her desires—reborn her—she my child—I mother of mother." To live your mother's dream is to never let her go. After my mother's death, at eleven, I wore her old stockings to school, and in my sixties I relived her life in prose. After fleeing from your father, you went from one avant-garde circle of artists to another, from Berlin to Munich and eventually New York City. I also ran away from my father and found direction in a bohemian community in Detroit. Over the years, I would read whatever I could find about you in English—after all, you were an experimental artist, a fore-sister. You never had much money, working now and again, mostly as a model, and often begging from friends or stealing when needed. You were flamboyant, you were bawdy and erotic, you were dada before dada. You often pushed away, sometimes attacking, those from whom you wanted friendship or intimacy or help. You made art from found objects, your body a stage for wild costuming. You were experimental with punctuation, "your style rising out of heaps of fragments." In 2016, I adopted your dashes, making my daily poems move faster, more emphatic, the thoughts piling one on top of another. After WWI came to an end, many of your friends left New York for Paris, and you raised enough money to return to Germany. What a shock that must have been. After so much destruction and death, Berlin was not the same, neither were you. Unprepared for such extreme poverty, you must have been terribly lonely for physical contact with others. Sexual activity was once considered a remedy for melancholia. In your autobiography, you write, "Such lamentable lack of diplomacy in me… has brought me to my present ruin." In a letter to Peggy Guggenheim: "Account overdrawn. I had no balance." Friends sent money, but not enough. If dada is an affirmation of life and freedom, is suicide an option? That's the question you must have considered before you turned on the gas.

Left: Elsa von Freytag-Loringhoven (aka the Baroness) International News Photography (INP); right: Elsa's New York City studio, 1915, George Grantham Bain Collection, Library of Congress, WDC.

DIANE

I arrived in the East Village fifteen years behind you and your friends. In the early '70s, in Detroit's Cass Corridor, we were also inventing our lives with as much personal and artistic freedom as possible. Not just the men. Us, too, with our strollers. A thread, a continuity. After I wrote you asking for poems in *Long News,* for many years our postcards, books and letters went back and forth. Always encouraging, you wrote, "I take you your friendship your work seriously and want always to give you full attention. Love you. Diane di P." By October 2010, your health had taken a downturn, and you were carrying an oxygen tank when you came to New York to read. I introduced you and Judith Malina at the Living Theater. On my shelf, a very ethereal-looking photo of you and me taken in the dark. When Maureen and I planned to stop and see you in the nursing home, you cautioned us because there was a flu that month. The year before Covid, we weren't concerned. On the altar in your room: Buddha, Trungpa, a Poetry Project newsletter, a windmill and a few spiritual books. In the photo, a mirror behind the altar, my image looks back with the camera. You couldn't move your legs. I sent you a bottle of mahanarayana healing oil. I wanted to help, but by then not possible. Bedridden, still you laughed and talked about your new book, *Spring and Autumn Annals*—each paragraph a poem, revealing the joys, trauma and losses of living artistically on the edge with children. A poem, a history, a map of a place, time and people. Dedicated to your dear friend, Freddie Herko. "Beauty is truth, truth beauty,—that is all / Ye know on earth, and all ye need to know." You loved Keats. Much truth here, much to give. From Hunter College to Poet Laureate of San Francisco. All for beauty, truth, and love, big love.

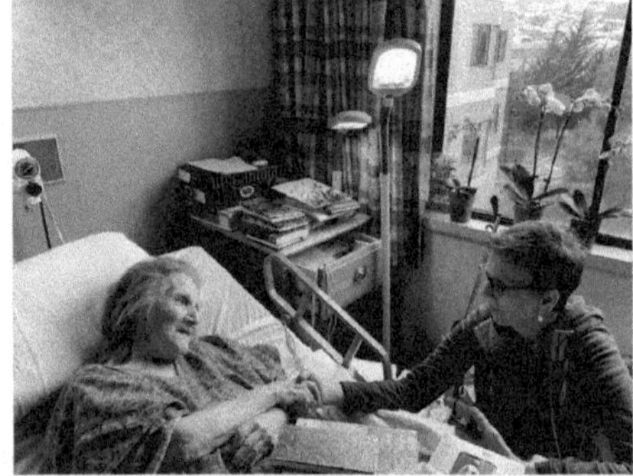

Left: Diane di Prima and Barbara at The Living Theater, Oct 20, 2010, photo by Dumisani Kambi-Shamba; right: Diane and Barbara, 2019, Jewish Home for the Aged in San Francisco, photo by Maureen Owen.

ESTHER

Your mother was a hairdresser and your father worked for your uncle's cigar company. You grew up in Boston, an only child in a Jewish family. Ten years behind you, I grew up in a midwestern working-class Protestant family. Neither of us were religious. You defended me when I was attacked in a tenure review. Often, we'd meet at Café Orlin in the East Village halfway between my apartment and yours. You encouraged me to love D— and then later to leave him. He thought we had something sexual going on because you were a lesbian and we cared about each other. I laughed. We can be friends, too, you know, I said to him. When I was living in Tucson, we talked on the phone most nights. We still talk on the phone most nights. When I was ill and lost my voice, you met me in the doctor's office. You have been like a sister to me. When you were seventy, to help an Afghan woman keep her child and escape a frightening husband, you climbed down a ravine, hid her in the bushes and then took her where she could declare asylum and live in safety with her child. Besides being a professor, you built a six-sided house, worked as a carpenter, an artist, a filmmaker, and a social activist helping women in Afghanistan. When Covid hit the city, you caught the first wave and your issues with memory became worse. Now when you lie down on the doctor's table, you get dizzy. "I'm so worried," you say. "I'm forgetting more and more. I can't remember anything." You used to boldly walk against traffic and into the middle of the intersection, but now I reach out and try—difficult as it might be—to guide you across with the light.

Esther Hyneman in her studio, early '90s.

KÄTHE

> *The worst of it all is that every war already carries within it the war which will answer it. Every war is answered by a new war, until everything, everything is smashed.... That is why I am wholeheartedly for a radical end to this madness.*
> (Letter to Ottilie, Feb 21, 1944)

New Year's Day 2024. With everyday news of more war deaths in the Ukraine and in Israel/Palestine, I sit quietly with your writing and prints. My generation also suffered from war loss—in Vietnam my brother was shot and my first boyfriend lost both his legs. I first saw one of your self-portraits in the German Expressionist room at the DIA, maybe in '73, and I've kept your work near me ever since. The loss in your face reminds me of my Swiss grandmother who came to help my father take care of us after our mother died. You were born in 1867, my grandmother was born in 1894, young enough to be your daughter. In response to loss, she crocheted, gardened and cooked. I watched her turn inward as her body collapsed in the chair in our living room. After your son Peter was killed in World War I, you wrote in your diary, "Then came the war and turned everything topsy-turvey. Knocked down flat on the ground. Half alive and half dead, one crawled in silence, living a humble life drenched with suffering. One rose to one's feet very slowly." You worked through your grief with your art, art for the public, print media and two stunning sculptures of grieving parents installed at the war cemetery in Flanders. Your husband was a doctor serving workers in a clinic in your house in Berlin. As those who were poorly paid and lived under harsh conditions came and left, you counseled and sketched them. Because of your anti-war art-activism, the Nazis refused to let you show your work anywhere or teach for the rest of your life. After the Gestapo came to your house, you and Karl carried vials of poison in case they tried to arrest you. In your woodcut, "The Mothers," the women form a circle wrapping their arms around their children, as if to say, *You will not have them. War. Death. We will die with them. In unity. They will not be torn from us.* In the shape of a tombstone. Then you lost a grandson in World War II and a few weeks before Germany surrendered, you died. Your son, Hans, describes you in his last visit. "Shattered by age though she was, she seemed like a queen in exile; she had a compelling kindliness and dignity." In your lithograph, "The Call of Death," Death taps you on the shoulder. Her hand is delicate. Your hand is suspended as if in the middle of saying something to someone. You turn and look over your shoulder. *Oh, it is only you...*

Left: Käthe Kollwitz, 1928, photo by Emil Hoppe; right: "The Mothers," woodcut, 1922-23.

HARRYETTE

Lorenzo Thomas and I stopped by the Nuyorican Poets Cafe. You were there with your sister Kirsten. "You should ask Harryette for work for *Long News,*" he said. "Her book, *Trimmings* is wonderful." I loved the dance of fragments, the playfulness, the celebration of femininity, experimental, language luscious and politically charged. For some reason, you and I hit it off immediately. We almost bought an old adobe house together in Las Vegas, New Mexico. But the town was so small. Could I find work there? My children and friends were in New York. Would I like it? Would it need a lot of repairs? A second home for you, but my primary space. I could never go back home to New York if I owned a house out west, and I've always liked moving around. Eventually, I chickened out. In 2009, we talked for hours on the phone about the poems in *Sleeping with the Dictionary,* and we turned our talks into a book. Once I stayed with you in LA. We cruised the city photographing for the book—the Crenshaw neighborhood, Robert Graham's sculpture garden at UCLA, Watts Towers. When I recall your house, I think of burgundy. Is that a favorite color? Many meetings over the years as we crisscrossed the country, and long periods of silence, too. Then someone stirs my memory with an email, like last week—Do you know how I can reach Harryette Mullen?—so I send you a text and you call me back. And we catch up as if no time has passed.

Harryette Mullen and Barbara: Brooklyn, May 7, 2024.

EMILY

When I was a child, we read your poems for children, the celebration of the train lapping up the miles, that type of thing. Back then, I didn't realize that your poems could be so dark, written to the rhythm of the hymns we would sing in church. As an adult, I found your unedited poetic voice beyond chilling. Awe. Stuttering awe. With a scratchy cough-damaged voice, I once sang your poem for my students—"Because I could not stop for Death / He kindly stopped for me"—as if a stanza of "Amazing Grace." A Brooklyn gospel singer picked up where I left off. Today it's fall and the leaves scatter. Awake, I think of winter coming, how the earth has a span of life, too, a beginning and an end. Me, here in this bed, so small on this planet that's spinning along on its own course, all of us part of the immense distance. A friend lies down this morning under a scalpel. The driver, the chariot, the horses gallop forward. Ding, ding, an email—*K's in recovery, doing well.* We gather in your garden, in your poem, with you, Emily, studying a Bee on a Clover Plank. Just as a crack opens in our view, the Bee is swept away with the Wind, and without a Moment to Spare, we are close behind.

Emily Dickinson, daguerreotype, 16 years old, approx.1846.

LORINE

When I was a child, we used to camp on the Keweenaw Peninsula, the uppermost peak of Michigan jutting out into Lake Superior. As an adult, I spent months at my sister's place writing a novel that took place near the lake, and many times I've taught your poem, *Lake Superior*, as an objectivist project; in the poem you pay tribute to the minerals in our bodies, in the rocks, the bed of the lake and the surrounding shore. As the only woman identified with the Objectivist poets, you had a lifelong correspondence and friendship with Louis Zukofsky, and when you were in your thirties, you and he were intimates. Reading your biography, I felt protective of you and upset with him (even though I had dedicated a book to him) for insisting you throw out all letters revealing your personal relationship, a decade of correspondence. And he insisted you have an abortion when you didn't want one, even though you were willing to raise the child on your own. Everything into the flood. Zukofsky was a New Yorker. Most of your life you lived on a watery island in rural Wisconsin. You also worked in a library, for the Federal Writer's Project, then proofreading, but because of your declining eyesight, that too, came to an end. Your last job was working in a hospital, as a cleaning woman. At sixty, your marriage to Albert Millen allowed you to write full time and let loose with your own hybrid poetics—objective, subjective and sometimes surreal. What I love most about your poetry, especially the later poems, is the way you engage the reader in a narrative or in particulars and then a rupture, a splinter, and another, and you take us elsewhere, sometimes into a spiritual awareness of our relational mortality, akin to Emerson or Whitman—"*Museum* // Having met the protozoic / Vorticellae / here is man / Leafing toward you / in this dark / deciduous hall." You once explained to a friend, "I looked back of our buildings to the lake and said, 'I am what I am because of all this—I am what is around me—those woods have made me.'" According to Margot Peters, Charles Olson admired your work, but you were not so hot about his. Both of your poetics were rooted in place. Living on an island, for you, water was everywhere. "O my floating life / Do not save love / for things // throw things / to the flood". When I revisited my copy of *The Granite Pail,* I found a penciled note in the margin: "In my poem!" I searched through my books. "Aren't These Lilies Lovely" was written in '93 when I was staying with a friend in Provincetown. I must have written "Throw things to the flood" in the corner of a journal and then collaged it into my own work, forgetting where it had come from. Now and forever, a line from your poem is intertwined with mine.

Lorine Niedecker on Black Hawk Island. Courtesy of the
Hoard Historical Museum and Fort Atkinson Historical Society (Wisconsin).

LISA

I used to see you and your Doberman in the East Village, two elegant tall beings strutting down the street, side by side, heads lifted. You sat on the back of my scooter cutting across Mysore with a bouquet of flowers for your guru. One evening in Tucson, we were walking your newly adopted dog, Ratna, and as he sniffed here and there, I pointed to the clouds and the white moon, a moment of spontaneous meditation. In swishy skirts and jazz shoes, we danced swing at the armory. A young man with a straw hat and suspenders winked at me and we started to lindy hop. Wow—to be young forever—he twirled me around so fast and so low that I started to lose my breath, my heart pounding. When the band stopped, I bowed and ran to the bathroom to let my lungs recover, and you were also there recovering your breath. Once we were eating popcorn and watching *Harold and Maude,* a story about a young man who falls in love with a quirky, honest, crazy loving-life older woman. You looked at me funny, as if to say, Barbara, why don't you find yourself a Harold. In 2012, I was back in New York, but after a surgery, I stayed with you in Tucson for a few days, glad for your ayurvedic cooking and massage. I remember driving your red pickup and riding your bicycle. How I love Tucson and love you, too, dear. When I had boyfriend-blues, you said, "You, know, Barb, you were happy before him, you were very happy." I needed to hear that. We have always been blunt with each other in our search for truth. "Better to set the good in stone and the negative in water," you suggested not long ago, and I replied, "Sometimes we repeat what we forget, so best to also keep an eye on the colors in the stream.

Left: Lisa Schrempp and Barbara, 2015, Tucson; right: Lisa and Bella, Phoenix, 2019.

GENNY

For years, once a week, I biked over to your class on Wooster Street. You wove together your asana instructions with metaphor and allusions to literature, art and philosophy. When I was traveling, as I passed over the Mackinac Bridge, I heard your voice, and I sat up straight in the driver's seat: "Lift your diaphragm, like delicately lifting a lady's handkerchief on two pillars dividing north from south." Even as we bent our bodies around chairs and blocks and hung from ropes, there was always a spiritual stillness in the room. Once because of a recent breakup, I was in tears, and you looked at me and then said to everyone, "Yoga is a healing art. It opens up blockages in the body just by doing it." Another time the elevator was out, and you carried my big suitcase up to your studio on the 5th floor. I was huffing and puffing behind you. In an email you once wrote: "People like us, with a kyphotic thoracic spine, need to move the spinous processes—those stegosaurus-like projections off the back of the vertebrae—move them in and slightly up and then we experience length and ease." Yesterday when I took your pranayama class on zoom, I noticed that, like me, you were forgetting this and that. A few months earlier, your collarbone was healing, now your wrist is injured. Afterwards, you stayed on to talk to me about aging and my tightening knees. You assured me we all get stiff with age, and we are both in our seventies. As I said goodbye to you for your vacation, I could feel you moving away from us. One day, I hope long into the future, you will say you are not going to teach anymore and that thought makes me very sad.

Left: Genny Kapuler in her studio, March 3, 2010, photo by Barbara; right: Genny and Barbara at the Poetry Project, Feb 29, 2012, photo by Michah Saperstein.

GLORIA

We met at the Kaveri Inn on a dirt road in the heart of Mysore. After morning yoga, cross-legged on the floor in front of the Ashtanga guru, Patthabi Jois, we rolled our eyes as he asked for chocolate and American money. You spoke Spanish but knew some English. I spoke a little Spanish. In the Indian restaurants while eating idli and curry, we pretended we were in Paris. You had married a Frenchman once and lived in Paris as a dancer. I had just broken up with a philosopher who loved everything French. You could walk right into the most frightening Indian traffic and the vehicles and cows would weave around you. You made a sculpture in the courtyard with Indian artists who were carving statues of Hindu gods. In Puerto Vallarta, I visited you and we swam with the crabs, went to your art openings, traveled with your boyfriend into the countryside, and fasted on black grapes. I took your yoga classes and wrote about you in a photo poem pamphlet. I gave you a copy, but I was never sure if you liked it or not. A poetic word collage can make for misunderstanding. After I moved to Tucson, you called me on Christmas Eve from your parents' house in Nogales. You wanted to talk, and when I was home, I tried to call you back, but after that, I couldn't get a line through. For two days I couldn't get through. And then you were gone. Too many people calling from Tucson to Mexico on Christmas. Perhaps you thought I was dissing you. Inadvertently offensive. A translator needed. Many translators. No response. Tangled lines. And that's how we lost each other.

Barbara and Gloria, 2003, Puerto Vallarta.

MIRANDA

When you moved from Detroit to New York, you volunteered to help with *Long News* and then you became the art editor. We spent weekends in the galleries looking for visuals and talking about theory and politics. You made covers for many of my books—a spooky Dürer engraving of a devilish guy with a skull coat of arms and wings tempting a woman with carnal pleasure; in shadow a woman (isn't that you?) photographing a tree with an open book in the branches; in the corridor between your house and your neighbor's, dark blurry figures strolling forward and back. Once you were collecting objects that held guilt, a ritual project—a Mother's Day card that Allen had given me after we broke up; I'd behaved badly and thrown it at him. I've always felt guilty about this. Even after you cut it up and burned it, I still felt guilty. I remember once lying on my bed calling stores and restaurants to try and find a pair of lost glasses, while you photographed my belly button for some project. You clipped 999 corners from my books, and I collected a line from each one, making 72 sonnets, *My Autobiography*. A triptych of your bird nests is on my wall. In the mid '90s, you started practicing Ninjutsu and I started with Ashtanga yoga. You tried to help me with my difficult cough, teaching me some qigong breathing. You loved my dog Dorothy, and you took a photo of us for the cover of *Me & My Dog*. You've always been an animal lover. Several lost cats have found home with you. We've both had a lot of losses over the years, and a couple of minor fallings out. Even though once in a while we make each other crazy, we've worked together on many projects, and not long ago, we promised each other to stay friends forever.

Left: Dorothy and Miranda Maher, 1999, photo by Barbara; middle and right: two of many book covers designed by Miranda.

SYLVIA

On retreat in Chappaquiddick, I did my first headstand on a porch right beside you. At 6 a.m., we'd meet on the corner of Avenue A and 7th Street and ride our bikes over to Eddie's yoga shala in Soho. You're a world traveler, back and forth to LA where you were born, to India, Latin America and Europe. When you started teaching yoga, at first you volunteered helping those who couldn't afford the high price for studio yoga. Once I subbed for you in a rehab center on Avenue C. Eventually you took a full-time gig, your life-dharma, I think, in a middle school teaching young teens. When my tiny studio was crowded with others, you let me use your apartment to work on my novel. In trade, I helped you with stories you were writing. When bedbugs invaded my apartment, we talked into the night, you on your bed tucked into the corner and me a few feet away in the living area. Often on my way home, I'd cut down 9th Street, look up and see you pass across the red curtain in your apartment. I'd holler up and you'd buzz me in. We used to live right around the corner from each other. Last month, I took the train in from Brooklyn to meet you at Divvy's on 1st Ave. As I sat across the table from you, I felt so much love. The earth seems to be spinning around faster each year and before we know it, another five years will pass. How I used to love coming around a corner in the East Village or around an aisle in Commodities, and there you'd be. "Hey you," I'd say and give you a big hug.

Left: Sylvia Rascon, Tompkins Sq, 2003, photo by Barbara; right: Dorothy, Sylvia and Barbara, 2000, 7th Street apartment, photo by neighbor.

JULIE

One hot night in 2010, we met for tea. You talked of an acupuncturist who had helped your mother with her breathing. I made an appointment and then he and I were involved for five years, living together in my small studio with his young son. When you were out of town, I found a quiet retreat in your apartment. Sometimes you came over for dinner with us. When we broke up, you consoled me. One of your collages is on my living room wall, a dress with leaves and bits of flowers and odds and ends, antlers for straps, with no head but ankles and shoes, as if a fairy had hung up her dress in the field. Once in your place in Cleveland, I stood at the window looking down on you in your garden, chatting with neighbors and tending to the plants. I took photos of your artwork, found objects and sculptures made from discarded junk. Everything about your life is part of your art. I talked to the Belladonna board about how wonderful your emails were, that we should make a book of them. I photographed you at several readings, and we read together in Detroit a few times. In your sensuous improvs (*making-do* you call it), you pull words, syllables and phrases right out of the air, like scatting, some jazzy hybrid between song and poem. Some poets struggle for a line, but not you. For you, everything bumps against everything else and blossoms into something different. Open an old refrigerator and you'll find a flower garden. After you gave up your apartment in the city, on my travels back and forth from Detroit, I stopped a few times to hang out with you and Arcey. When Covid descended, our rhythms hesitated, not for a month but for a couple of years, and now we're older and I'm not doing much long distance driving anymore. I do miss seeing you. I open my last email from you, sent on September 18, 2021, and I laugh out loud.
Barbara! I squeeze you tight with all my might
And catch you in New York soon soon swoon
Before the shivery moon
Love you!

Julie Ezelle Patton, Center for Book Arts, Nov 14, 2012.
Photo by Barbara.

MAUREEN

In '88 Lewis asked you to write a blurb for my first book, *Smoking in the Twilight Bar.* Over the years, we hung out at poetry readings in New York, Tucson and in Boulder. While we were teaching for Naropa, we talked on the phone for hours. The year before the pandemic, in our seventies (both with grown children, and grandchildren), we circled the country on a reading tour. I taught you yoga, and even though I try to be optimistic, I had to keep up with you, especially in Albuquerque when my lungs didn't like the altitude, the cold air and the dirty hostel where we were staying. I couldn't breathe, and you helped me carry things upstairs. You could stay up all night talking about poetry. Once we sat in the Walmart parking lot, making tempeh-tuna sandwiches on a cutting board, and we laughed at ourselves. Problems? Sure. Someone was always in a hurry, someone was irritable, someone was snoring, someone forgot to take a photo, someone said something to hurt the other, someone needed to be alone, someone was cold and there weren't enough blankets, someone was worried about what was going on at home. But look at that mountain, that cloud formation, the wind turbines, those poor cows corralled like that, clink clunk, someone's shoulder caught in a cramp, someone wants to eat real food, someone wants to kill the bully, but someone is a pacifist, someone needs to write alone, someone needs to be alone. Now I call you up if I can't think of the right word. I say that all my relatives died around my age, and you advise, that's not the way to think about it, Barb. I had trouble sleeping, but you could fall asleep anywhere. Two months in a car and fifteen poetry readings later, at the end of the trip, I was camping out in the room in your basement. When I went upstairs to ask you a question, you were in a U shape on the sofa, sound asleep. Another time, you were leaning on your mother as she gazed out the window, sound asleep. What a gift, to be able to sleep like that.

Maureen Owen and Barbara, 2007, Mission San Xavier del Bac Cemetery. Photo by Laynie Brown.

MARTINE

I met you in the '90s after publishing a poem of yours in *Long News*—mythic, spiritual, experimental, a narrative repeating, transforming. I remember sitting together at the Nuyorican Poets Cafe. When I sent my interviews of Harryette Mullen to *Belladonna,* you volunteered to edit the book, and we worked together closely on the project. After spending so much time discussing Oulipo, we decided to write a series of poems together. 14 lines a day for 14 days on 4 x 6 cards, later published together in *Peep/Show.* I visited you a couple times out in Montauk in the summer. I remember taking HD's *Notes on Thought & Vision* off your shelf and reading some of it to you while we sat on the beach. "The love-mind and the over-mind... properly adjusted, focused, they bring the world of vision into consciousness." We read together once with Rachel Levitsky at the hidden library on Jersey Street. The last time I saw you, you were reading your poems online for Tucson's Poetry Group, and then before that, reading parts of my novel for the *Brooklyn Rail.* Before Covid hit the city, made all the poetry readings take place on zoom, and kept us home alone with Criterion, we used to meet for dinner and films. For some reason *Melancholia* stays in my mind, the planet heading toward earth, the end imminent and everyone praying and preparing. As we walked back to the East Village, we kept looking up at the sky. Once when I was hesitant about getting involved with someone because he had a child and I'd already raised two children, you said something profound, sharing your Buddhist knowledge with me—You never know, Barbara, that child might become the most important person in your life. Eventually, I lost the child, or he lost me, but if you had not said these words, I might never have loved in the way I loved.

Barbara and Martine Bellen at the Poetry Project, June 23, 2010.
Photo by Michah Saperstein.

JANE

Harry Mathews wrote me a letter in 2011 comparing my novella, "The Dinner" to your *Two Serious Ladies.* About your book, he wrote, "It's one of the brightest stars in my constellation of masterpieces." About mine, "It's an utterly captivating work (captivating = gripping, entertaining, impossible to stop reading, compelling, nifty)." In your novel, your characters make U-turns and zigzags. In your letters you ridicule your own suffering and indecision, and you seem unable to come to a decision about the most insignificant issues, constantly overwhelmed by multiple possibilities. You loved women, yet always deferred to Paul. His writing came first, and you were very insecure about your own. But your writing is so splendid. To decline. To be less than needed. To fall short. After a while, your friends became embarrassed you might lose control. When you were a grown woman, trying to hold on to your sanity, your mother called you "my little princess." After you died, the doctor explained, "For her it was fatal, the early life of pleasure, the drinking, the excitement, given her sensibility." As I'm driving on I-10—the big trucks and trains passing by, far distant horizon and jagged mountains—I think about you, like a child, but an adult. Maybe things would have been different if you had not always been provided for, maybe if you had to make a living and provide for others. I wonder if there aren't some benefits to economic necessity.

Jane Bowles. Photo by Rodrigo Rey Rosa.

BOBBIE LOUISE

Your grandmother once said to you, "You don't have to be ashamed of having ignorance or lice, Bobbie, you just have to be ashamed of keeping them." In the same year I was born, you packed up and left home to live with your first husband, Olaf, off on an adventure to Denmark, London and Belize. In *One Small Saga*, you write about a nineteen-year-old girl who's whisked away from her working-class life in West Texas by a well-to-do architect to live in London and then in Belise. "There's no such thing as fiction, It's all autobiography," you say. The narrator in Saga is so cool she plays down her own heartbreak. Instead of romanticizing the story, she sizes up those around her, with an understated poetic style and an eye especially sensitive to hypocrisy. When you were married to Bob Creeley, you and he drove to Guatemala with your children. In *The Sanguine Breast of Margaret*, poverty is simply a bothersome side effect of a bohemian adventure. What a lot of work when Margaret is on the road in a broken-down van with small children and not enough money to get to where they're going, washing diapers in roadside bathrooms. My children's father and I once drove down to Florida pulling a trailer with our two children and another child along for the journey, one in diapers. I know what that's like. Sweaty and smelly discomfort, but moments of beauty, too. You write, "Driving in the darkest small hours of the morning oncoming headlights would splay out across the wet windshield like exploding stars." I met you when you were 81 and I was 62. I spent a year interviewing, transcribing and helping you get your *Selected Prose* into the world. "Make yourself the editor," you insisted. "After all, you've already done the work." That year my dreams were interwoven with your stories. I remember wobbling over to the post office with my bike weighted down with 20 review copies of your *Selected Prose.* In the closing event at Naropa, with an oxygen tank nearby, you read dramatically with a Texas drawl a story about your mother explaining how to cook liver. The auditorium rolled with laughter. One summer, when your house was in the process of being dismantled, books stacked everywhere, you were moving into assisted living, and you urged me to take any books I wanted. You handed me Edward Dahlberg's *Because I Was Flesh.* I love that book, and I like holding it and knowing you read the same pages.

Bobbie Louise Hawkins, Placitas NM, early 1960s.

NANCY

For my ex-partner, the word "boyfriend" signaled disrespect. I had not experienced racism as he had. For me the word was looser and more joyous than partner or man friend; it was intimate, the child in the man. A minor difference, one word, but in our five years together, there were paragraphs, chapters and volumes. Many loving moments, of course, but after a while I couldn't calmly respond to his mood swings. I needed help. You were my age, single, sensible, years of experience as a psychotherapist, and hip at the same time. We had practiced yoga with the same teacher, and we knew many of the same people. Quickly, you picked up on what I already knew. Even though I loved him, I couldn't take a chance that seemed so slim, and instead end up ruining my final years. You helped me sort out many of my mother-loss reactions and fears. I would have left eventually, but I was relieved to have you at my back, helping me. You read my books as I was writing them. You came to my book party for *Just Like That.* You're still there for me when I'm in a quandary or I lose my cool and I'm blown around by my emotions. You understand what it's like to lose someone; you had two sons; one died when he was a young adult from an autoimmune illness. You know what it's like to live with a respiratory illness like mine. I'd bike uptown on 1st Avenue to your office, and we'd sit together with your puppy curled up at my feet. Now if we talk, it's on zoom. We often wavered over the line between friendship and therapy. For a while, I did your accounting and gave you yoga privates. When my son's wife was suicidal, you met with them, but she refused to return. A few years later, when she took her own life, you were there, without hesitation, for my son. You became his therapist and spiritual guide. Om Nama Shivaya. From one mother to another, Namaste.

Nancy Arann and Esther Hyneman at a book party for *Just Like That,* May 6, 2018. Photo by Orion Brown.

ELENA

During the terrible Covid year, you were the only person who touched my body. After my shoulder injury, you carefully realigned my shoulders. For the first time I realized where they were meant to be, back there on my back and not curling around toward the computer. While you work on me, we catch up, talking about what's happening in the news, events with neighbors, our families and what we've been cooking (you are an excellent cook, especially with the Italian food you grew up with). You went to Long Island University back in the early '80s for undergrad work, playing tennis and taking lots of lit courses. A friend and colleague I worked with for many years turned you on to theater and that became a life-long love for you. You still play tennis, and you like to bike and play with your neighbor's children at the beach near your home in Breezy Point. You wept when I told you that my son's wife had taken her life. We wept together. Even though you are my doctor, I think of you as a close friend, an advisor in a way, an optimistic, love-life advisor. You scold me if I say things like "I've only got ten years left," or if I say "my body is falling apart," you correct me, like last week when you said, "Come on, you have the body of a fifty-year-old." But back then my body didn't get injured so easily and it didn't hurt this much. Today while I was lying face down with tens electrodes on my lower back, I heard another patient as he was leaving, "Thank you, Elena, You know—*Come si dice*—I'd come around the world to see *you.*"

Elena de Lucia, October 6, 2023. Photo by Barbara.

CARI

One day, I couldn't get to my yoga class on Wooster Street because a big snowstorm had blocked all the streets, so I went around the corner to Avenue B where a young man was teaching some strange postures—wild twists and backbends with every move. I loved Katonah yoga, so I started biking over to his teacher in Chelsea where later you and I used to practice side by side. When I moved back to Brooklyn, I looked around for a Katonah class, and I found you, teaching in four different places. I followed you from one place to the next. You tend to arrive just in the nick of time, and then run over the clock. I was often your timekeeper. You're a mother with a busy schedule, and you love whatever you're doing, so why stop. Like your teachers, Nevine and Abby, you realign and turn your students on metaphorically—the body is a house—the first floor our stability; the body is a car—the sex organ the ignition; the body is an instrument—you have to fine-tune it. We both like to talk. We talk to help each other through our difficulties and during the covid years, we had many—divorce, death, illness, and on and on. We talk to help find more joy and understanding in our lives. How I love running into you in the food co-op. Or when we make time to walk through the park with your dog Kula, like yesterday as the November yellow, orange and brown leaves were falling through the air and scattering around us. In midsummer, you instructed me on the edible plants in the park, but today we talk about our families and tasks to be done. Will I help your daughter with her essays? Yes, of course, anytime.

Left: Cari Friedman with Barbara on her 70th, Oct 26, 2018; right: Cari at Yoga & Yogini, Jan 19, 2023, photo by Michah Saperstein.

FERNE

You taught me how to fold towels and sheets. You taught me how to separate the dirty clothes into various piles. You taught me how to hang clothes on the clothesline. When you were taking care of our new baby, I took care of my baby doll. You taught me how to line up cans of soup in rows in the cupboard. You taught me how to clean the woodwork and you paid me two cents for each wall. You taught me how to cut out little circles and stitch along the edges, pulling them into pouches, then flattening and sewing them together. You invited all the little girls in the neighborhood to our quilting party. When I was very young, you were beautiful and energetic. When I was ten years old, you were weak and skinny to the bone. The phone was always ringing. You had three sisters and many friends. You were a Sunday School teacher and a Cub Scout den mother. Women in the neighborhood would come over for coffee; you'd chat, smoke and talk in the kitchen. When I was very young, we dressed up and played cocktail lounge on our coffee table. When I was a little older, you told me secrets about your life as if I was your friend—a first husband, your boyfriends, your discontent with my father. After winding my hair into pin curls, you patted my head and sent me to bed. When I was worried whether I really believed in God or not, you reassured me that if I was worried, then I had nothing to worry about. Be kind. Be helpful. Go to church. You taught me how to wash and dry dishes. How to boil a potato and mash it. How to make a hamburger. After you died, I'd pretend I was sick and stay home from school looking through photo albums and watching old movies from the '40s. I remember people talking about the size of the crowd at the funeral parlor. I remember hearing my father say, *They had to open another room for Fernie.* I refused to recognize the stepmother who arrived a year later with a very strict set of rules. No one could replace you. As an older adult, I researched your life and times and wrote a book about you. This morning, I realized I haven't been thinking about you that much lately, my life as a child now like a small shrinking room filled with blue sky, and I'm on my bike pedaling down the street. It's 20 degrees today. Outside my window the sun casts a light orange over the towering oak tree as its branches waver in the frigid air. The forecast for Tuesday is ten degrees warmer, then on Wednesday, even warmer.

Ferne Hostetter, 1941; Barbara, 1960

GINNY

You and Patti were always close; you grew up sharing a bedroom and later you both became nurses. Your life wasn't easy in our family. With the loss of our mother and then the arrival of a stepmother, as the child in the middle, you were often neglected. You weren't rebellious, except in minor ways, common to us all—eating all the Girl Scout cookies, kissing the boy down the street, cutting up Dick, Jane and Sally books. Once when you were about seven years old, you were angry, so you put some clothes in your doll's suitcase, hooked it up on your bike, announced you were running away, and then you rode around the block several times. Of the three of us, you were the first to get married and have a baby. I tried to help, but I had no experience with babies. When you had postpartum depression, I found you walking in a desolate area of the city. I brought you home with me. When I was pregnant and you were planning at the spur of the moment, an all-night drive down south with your baby to see a friend, I went with you. When our daughters became close, you often took my daughter overnight. We had our share of arguments, but none of them were long lasting. After we moved to New York, I was absent from most of the family gatherings. You stayed close to Dad and Jean, though, and when they were near the end, you did most of the work taking care of them, as daughter and nurse. You have an extended family in your duplex—you, your high school boyfriend lifelong husband, your daughter and grandson. Over the years, you've had a lot of trouble with your body, surgery on your ankles and your hip, auto-immune pain, but you have been resilient and humorous through it all. As children, all four of us took care of each other; and even if our lives are very different now, we are still there for each other.

Left: Ginny Henning, 1958; right: Ginny, Patti and Barbara, 1967.

PATTI

When I was nine and you were three, you followed me around and I'd say, Patti, get me that, do this, do that. When we were a bit older, and our mother was in the hospital, you thought I was your mother, but I was only a kid. I made up scary stories at night and you repeated them in kindergarten. Your teacher called me to her classroom to talk after school. She was worried. Would I tell my father about the stories? A few years later, our stepmother arrived, and I fought with her, but you were too young to fight. As a young teenager you took quaaludes and pretended you were tired. I begged you not to take them. One night I left home with a boyfriend. Soon after, Bobby went to Vietnam and Ginny got married. You were left behind with Jean who wouldn't let you wash your hair or your uniform for your part-time job as a nurse's aide in the hospital. It was as if she was living in the middle of the Depression, but there was no Depression, just a small envelope of power. You did well in school, played the guitar, went to Europe, then off to college as far away as you could go and still be in Michigan. Then you married and we both had babies. After Allen and I broke up, my children came to your house for holidays, and you took Michah in when he was a teenager and needed to get away from the city. You flew to New York to help me when Allen was dying. After your thirty-year marriage ended, you were lost for a while. You said you felt like a plant ripped out of the soil. You moved, retired, planted flowers, planted a lot of flowers, and then you found another job downstate. I liked being single and independent together with you, even just on the phone or in the summers, but now, five years later, you're back in the northern woods, moving with the winds of Lake Superior, married again, hiking and kayaking. When you were living alone, you used to say, "All of you, my brother and sisters, can come and live with me when you're old." But now we're getting old, living with our own histories, spread out and rooted in the places where we chose to go, many miles apart.

Left: Patti Henning with Barbara, 1962; right: 1976.

LINNÉE

After you were born, we bought an old house with a room for you with rose wallpaper. You loved reading and looking at books, but sometimes you were a little tot with attitude. You'd sit on the potty and demand more and more books to read. Your nursery school teacher said, "Tell her to get them herself." After that, you miraculously potty trained yourself. For three years you woke us up in the middle of the night wanting company, but on the day Michah was born, you both slept through the night. You two were always close, even though he used to tease you. Now you live with all boy energy, two teenage boys and a husband. As a child (and now as an adult) you were articulate, beautiful and vibrant. And you always loved to draw and paint. You stood up for yourself when you were wronged, and for your friends, too. As a teenager, you were impatient with teachers who weren't really teaching, and now you're a middle-school teacher and a student advocate. You loved your kindergarten and first grade teacher, Mrs. Snyder. And your married name is Snyder! You're a do-er, like me, keep busy, take care of everyone. I worry sometimes that you don't take enough time for yourself.

You didn't like it when Dad and I split up, and we moved out of our house into two small apartments, and you didn't like it when I left you and Michah in Detroit, so I could look for an apartment and a job in New York. It was the only way I could resettle us. And in retrospect, I think it was the right thing to do. For a while we had to deal with tight funds, with me working so much, and then with Dad's illness. You didn't like a few of my boyfriends, and you were usually right on that account. Sometimes I was sad, sometimes irritable and short tempered, but I always loved you. I couldn't give you what you're giving your children, but I helped both of you make it through school, and if you got in trouble, I got you out of it, negotiating with teachers, finding new schools, talking with you to help solve your problems. Once you were reading Charlotte's Web and you wrote for your school assignment. "Her mother was a cooker. My mother is a writer." You probably got a lot of strengths from our alternative life—your creativity, your love of children and family, your call to teach, your outrage at unfairness. When Dad was dying, I played Louis Armstrong, "What a Wonderful World" and when you married Greg, you asked me to dance with you, in Dad's place, and you had the DJ play that same song. No matter the difficulties and losses in life, it is all so stunningly beautiful, isn't it? Remember when I took the train out to South Hampton to your dorm to bring you a pumpkin cheesecake for your birthday. And while I was there with you and your friends in the dorm, the phone rang two times. It was Dad checking up on you.

Linnée Saperstein Snyder. Top: Barbara and Linnée on Linnée's 3rd Birthday, (so happy with Mr. Potato); in back, Richie Hartigan, Allen Saperstein and Bob Henning; bottom: Barbara and Linnée, in Barbara's 7th Street apartment, 2002, photo by Michah Saperstein.

NOTES

Page 1. Barbara, 1957. Photo by Robert Henning.

Page 7. Laura Ingalls Wilder. *Little House in the Big Woods,* Harper, 1932; and *The Long Winter,* Harper, 1940.

Page 10. Louisa May Alcott. *Little Women,* Sea Wolf Press, 2020. Jo March is a character in Alcott's book.

Page 12. Emily Brontë (Catherine Earnshaw). *Wuthering Heights,* Penguin Classics, 2003, 82. Catherine Earnshaw is the female protagonist in Brontë's book.

Page 15. Barbara, photo, 1967.

Page 27. Jean Rhys. (1) *Good Morning Midnight,* Bantam Classic, 1983. (2) Emily Dickinson, "Good Morning — Midnight —" #425, *The Complete Poems of Emily Dickinson,* Ed., Thomas H. Johnson, Little Brown, 203. (3) Jean Rhys, *Smile Please: An Unfinished Autobiography,* Penguin, 1979, 103.

Page 28. Faye Kicknosway. (1) Francis Ponge, *Soap,* Lane Dunlope, Trans., Jonathan Cape Ltd., 1969. (2) *A Man is a Hook. Trouble,* Capra Press, 1974.

Page 29. Harriette Hartigan. June Singer, *Androgyny: Toward a New Theory of Sexuality,* Anchor Press/Doubleday, 1977.

Page 31. Michah, Linnée and Barbara, photo by Allen Saperstein, 1983.

Page 37. Esther M. Broner. (1) *Her Mothers.* Holt Rhinehart Winston, 1975. (2) Phyllis Chesler. *Diary of Motherhood,* T.Y. Crowell, 1979.

Page 38. Nancy Armstrong. *Desire and Domestic Fiction: A Political History of the Novel,* Oxford University Press, 1990.

Page 39. Virginia Woolf. (1) *To the Lighthouse,* Harcourt Brace Jovanovich, 1981. (2) "A Sketch of the Past," *Moments of Being,* Houghton Mifflin Harcourt, 81. (3) "A Sketch of the Past," 98.

Page 42. Grace Paley. (1) *Enormous Changes at the Last Minute,* Farrar, Straus and Giroux, 1985. (2) "Two Ears, Three Lucks," *The Collected Stories of Grace Paley,* Farrar, Straus and Giroux, 1994, x. (3) "A Subject of Childhood," *The Collected Stories,* 94-95 (originally in *The Little Disturbances of Man,* 1959).

Page 43. Karen Lemming. A line from Aretha Franklin's "Tiny Sparrow;" the song originated as an Appalachian folk ballad.

Page 45. H.D. (Hilda Doolittle). (1) Barbara Guest, *Herself Defined: the Poet H.D. and Her World,* Doubleday, 1984, 10. (2) H.D., *Trilogy,* New Directions, 1973, 37.

Page 47. Barbara, photo by Esther Chambers, 1994.

Page 49. Marguerite Duras. (1) *The Lover,* Random House, 1985, 55. (2) *The Lover,* 86.

Page 52. Marie Scavetta. Michel Foucault. *Discipline and Punish: the Birth of the Prison,* Alan Sheridan, Trans., Vintage Books, 1995.

Page 53. Mina Loy. (1) "Hot Cross Bum," *The Lost Lunar Baedeker Poems,* Farrar Straus Giroux, 1996, 133-144; (2) Carolyn Burke, *Becoming Modern: The Life of Mina Loy,* Picador, 1996, 178. (2) *Becoming,* 430.

Page 55. Julia Kristeva. *Black Sun: Depression and Melancholia,* Trans. Leon S. Roudiez, Columbia University Press, 1989, 151.

Page 58. Elsa Von Freytag-Loringhoven. (1) "The Baroness Begs for Help from Germany," 18 Page Letter to Mary Reynolds Fitzgerald, 1924. https://baronesselsa.org/items/show/22/. (2) Irene Gammel. *Baroness Elsa: Gender, Dada and Everyday Modernity.* MIT Press, 2002, 233. (3) Autobiography (typed manuscript), Ed. Tanya Clement. 81 of 220. http://www.baronesselsa.org/teibp/content/Auto.xml Accessed 8/2023. (4) *Body Sweats: The Uncensored Writings of Elsa Von Freytag Loringhoven,* Eds. Irene Gammel and Suzanne Zelazo, MIT, 2012. 276.

Page 60. Diane di Prima. (1) Letter to Barbara Henning, May 1, 2010. Beinecke Rare Book and Manuscript Library, Barbara Henning papers, b. 11, f. 287. (2) *Spring and Autumn Annals,* City Light Books, 2021. (3) John Keats, "Ode on a

Grecian Urn," first published anonymously in *Annals of the Fine Arts for 1819.*

Page 62. Käthe Kollwitz. (1) "Letter to Ottile, Feb 21, 1944," *The Diaries and Letters of Käthe Kollwitz,* Hans Kollwitz, ed., Henry Regency Co., Chicago, 1955, 184. (2) "New Years Eve, 1925," *The Diaries…,* 111. (3) Hans Kollwitz, "Introduction," *The Diaries…,* 11.

Page 64. Harryette Mullen. *Sleeping with the Dictionary,* University of California Press, 2002.

Page 65. Barbara, photo by Michah Saperstein, 2009.

Page 67. Emily Dickinson. (1) "Because I Could Not Stop for Death," (#712), *The Complete Poems of Emily Dickinson,* Ed., Thomas H. Johnson, Little Brown, 350. (2) Words taken from "A Single Clover Leaf," (#1343), 381.

Page 68. Lorine Niedecker. (1)"Traces of Living Things," *The Granite Pail,* North Point Press, 63. "Protozoic vorticellae" is a microscopic organism with stalks and tulip like bulbs. (2) Margot Peters. *Lorine Niedecker: A Poet's Life.* University of Wisconsin Press, 2011. Ebook. Chapter 22. (3) Lorine Niedecker, "Paean to Place," *The Granite Pail, 75.*

Page 78. Jane Bowles. (1) *Two Serious Ladies,* Sort of Books, 2000. (2) Harry Mathews, email to Barbara, Jan. 20, 2011, Beinecke Rare Book and Manuscript Library, Barbara Henning papers, YCAL MSS 1303, b.12, f. 358. (3) Millicent Dillon, ed., *Out in the World: Selected Letters of Jane Bowles 1935-1970.* (4) Millicent Dillon, *A Little Original Sin: The Life and work of Jane Bowles,* Holt, Rinehart and Winston, 1981.

Page 79. Bobbie Louise Hawkins. (1) Interview," *Selected Prose of Bobbie Louise Hawkins,* Ed., Barbara Henning, BlazeVOX, 2012, 378. (2) Selected Prose," Interview, 365. (3) *The Sanguine Breast of Margaret,* North and South, 1992, 23.

Page 83. Barbara in Mogador Café, photo by Michah Saperstein, 2014.

AUTHOR BIOGRAPHY

Barbara Henning is the author of eight collections of poetry, four novels and a book of creative non-fiction, *Ferne, a Detroit Story,* for which she received a Notable Book award from the Library of Michigan in 2023. Other recent publications include a novel, *Just Like That* (Spuyten Duyvil 2018); poetry collections, *Digigram* (United Artist Books 2020) and *A Day Like Today* (Negative Capability Press 2015); and *Prompt Book: Experiments for Writing Poetry and Fiction* (Spuyten Duyvil 2020). Barbara has taught for Wayne State University, Queens College, Naropa University and Long Island University where she is Professor Emerita. Born in Detroit, she presently lives in Brooklyn. More information is available on her website: www.barbarahenning.com.